For dearest Mum on
her birthday,
with our love,
    Richard & Ann,
        Kate & Lucy.

Jan. 1988.

The National Trust
Book of
TUCK BOX TREATS

Geraldene Holt

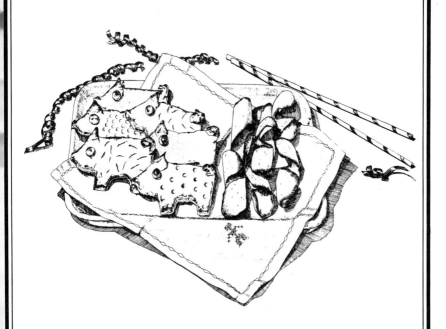

DAVID & CHARLES
Newton Abbot   London   North Pomfret (Vt)

FOR CHLOE, SAM AND KATHY,
SASHA, LUKE AND DANIEL

*refers to places owned by the National Trust
NB All spoon measures given in the recipes are level

British Library Cataloguing in Publication Data

Holt, Geraldene
  The National Trust book of tuck box
  treats.
  1. Pastry
  I. Title
  641.8'65   TX773

  ISBN 0-7153-9007-4

Typeset by ABM Typographics Limited, Hull
Printed in Great Britain
by Redwood Burn Limited, Trowbridge, Wilts
for David & Charles Publishers plc
Brunel House   Newton Abbot   Devon

Published in the United States of America
by David & Charles Inc
North Pomfret   Vermont 05053   USA

·Contents·

*Florence White's 'Really Delicious'
Chocolate Cake (p. 33)*

·Introduction·

This book is a collection of recipes of particular interest to children. It includes recipes which are favourites of children of today and of the past. However, the book is not aimed solely at children; many adults still hanker after the food they remember so vividly from their childhood which has so many happy associations for them. Who can forget that square of sticky gingerbread eaten in the privacy of one's bedroom; or a dark, rich, chocolate cake, cut clumsily with an old knife but shared amid happy laughter with school chums? Many will remember looking forward to the weekly outing to the village shop in order to choose from the tall, glass jars of sweets full of striped gobstoppers, satin cushions of humbugs flavoured with winter-green, or those flat slabs of chewy toffee that were shattered into bite-sized pieces by the shopkeeper's small, metal hammer.

This is true nostalgia food and I hope that this book will help you to recreate these treats, perhaps for your own children, your grandchildren or even yourself. While working on this book I have been reminded on many occasions of just how fond we were of these childhood treats. I have seen treasured recipes handed down from generation to generation, thereby maintaining long-established traditions. I have been struck by the devotion the cooks of the past and the present displayed in taking immense care to produce the best in homebaking for their family and friends.

This book also traces the history of baking in Britain, explaining not only what foods were baked but also how, and why. Collecting the recipes has been fascinating and I wish to express my gratitude to my mother. My thanks go to Dudley Dodd — who thought of the book — and Sally Twiss of the National Trust and also to my family and many friends, notably Lucy and Charlie Pinney, Anthea and Kitty Secker, Fiona Gimson, Anne Collieu, Michael Pinney and Michael Smith, who have donated recipes, cookery books and shared their memories with me.

A wise Frenchman, Pierre de Pressac, once wrote, 'Reconstitution of the past is a delicate pleasure of which one should not be deprived.' This book endeavours to bring the past alive again.

· Scones, Teabreads ·
and Crumpets

We can never be quite sure when baking began. It was probably about the time when man became less nomadic, started settlements and began to farm. He grew grain which, after threshing and winnowing, was ground in a stone quern to produce flour. The flour was mixed with water and at first was boiled to make a kind of porridge. This mixture continued as *frumenty*, a country dish, until the nineteenth century. And, of course, the Scottish version of porridge made with oatmeal or rolled oats is still widely eaten today.

If roughly ground grain is mixed with water to make a stiff paste or dough and spread on a large stone that has been heated in an open fire the mixture will bake. The result is a form of unleavened bread rather like an oatcake. This can taste surprisingly good, as anyone knows who makes their own oatcakes. For centuries baking was carried out in this way. It is thought that yeast-risen bread was discovered some time later. Perhaps a little of the uncooked dough was left under a fruit-bearing tree. Some of the natural yeast from the fruit landed on the mixture with the result that the natural yeasts started to work, producing carbon dioxide in the mixture and making it froth and foam which, after baking, gives the characteristic holes in a yeast-risen loaf or cake.

For centuries baking was carried out in this way, on a bakestone heated in an open fire. After the Iron Age a circle of cast iron replaced the stone. This was called a griddle or in some parts of Britain, a girdle. In Wales baking was carried out on a long metal shelf placed over the fire called a *plank*. Until the stone or brick-lined bread oven, built in the shape of a beehive, was introduced into larger houses and farmhouses, all baking was done over an open fire. A griddle was the only method available for baking. Sometimes the loaf on the griddle was covered with a metal hood or pan which enabled a larger loaf to be baked. A similar method is used for an Irish bannock (page 13).

Griddle scones, loaves, pancakes and crumpets are some of our oldest forms of baking. It is good to see that we still value this most traditional kind of home-baking. Many of these recipes like the Singing Hinnies of Northumbria or Scotch Pancakes are regional specialities. Others have been adapted for baking in the new ovens which were built into most people's houses from the middle of the nineteenth century onwards. Fat Rascals and Devonshire Splits are now baked in an oven but both started as griddle cakes.

Do not be put off if you have no griddle or girdle. Although it is still easy to buy a griddle — an old, blackened one in second-hand and antique shops, or a new gleaming one from a kitchen supplier — in most cases a heavy-grade, cast-iron frying pan works just as well for griddle baking. On the whole baking from the griddle is best eaten as soon as possible after cooking. This also applies to many of the scones in this chapter, a treacle scone is most delicious straight from the oven. Any scones or bread that remain uneaten are excellent toasted.

DEVONSHIRE · SPLITS · *(makes 12)*

These flat baps are served split in half, of course, with clotted cream and strawberry jam spooned in between. In Devon they are some-times filled with clotted cream and black treacle and are then called Thunder and Lightning.

1/2oz (15g) fresh yeast or 1 1/2 teaspoons (1 1/2 × 5ml) dried yeast
1 teaspoon (1 × 5ml) caster sugar
1/4pt (150ml) warm water
1lb (450g) plain flour
1/2 teaspoon (1/2 × 5ml) salt
1oz (30g) butter
1/4pt (150ml) milk
A little extra milk
Knob of butter

Cream the fresh yeast with the sugar and blend with the water. Alter-natively, sprinkle the dried yeast and sugar on to the water. Set the yeast mixture aside in a warm place for 10 minutes until frothy. Sieve the flour and salt into a bowl. Melt the butter in the milk and cool to lukewarm. Stir the milk and the yeast liquid into the flour and mix well for 3–4 minutes until the dough feels elastic. Cover the bowl with a loose plastic bag and leave in a warm place for 1 hour or until doubled in size. Turn the dough on to a floured board and knead lightly for 2 minutes. Cut the dough into 12 pieces and knead each piece into a ball. Flatten it until 1/2in (10mm) thick and place on a greased and floured baking sheet. Leave in a warm place for 20 minutes until puffy. Brush with milk and bake in a moderately hot oven (400°F, 200°C; Gas Mark 6) for about 20 minutes until golden brown. Transfer to a wire rack to cool and rub the knob of butter over the top of each bap while still warm.

SINGING · HINNIES

These griddle scones come from Northumberland. It is thought that their name arose from the 'singing' noise that the butter and cream make as they melt on the hot griddle while the scones cook.

8oz (225g) plain flour
1 teaspoon (1×5ml) baking powder
½ teaspoon (½×5ml) salt
4oz (115g) lard or half butter/half
    lard

2oz (55g) currants
½oz (15g) caster sugar
4 tablespoons (4×15ml) soured
    cream or double cream mixed
    with a squeeze of lemon juice

Sieve the flour, baking powder and salt into a bowl. Rub in the lard or mixture of lard and butter. Stir in the currants, sugar and soured cream to make a soft dough. Roll out on a floured surface to make one or two circles about ¼in (5mm) thick. Bake on a hot griddle for 6–8 minutes on each side. Serve warm, cut in wedges with butter, honey or jam.

SCOTCH · PANCAKES

These are the most famous Scottish drop scones. Try replacing the sugar with 2oz (55g) finely grated Cheddar cheese for a savoury flavour.

8oz (225g) self-raising flour
Good pinch of salt
2oz (55g) caster sugar

2 eggs
¼pt (150ml) milk
1oz (30g) butter, melted

Sieve the flour, salt and sugar into a bowl and beat in the eggs and milk to make a thick, smooth batter. Stir in the melted butter. Grease a hot griddle and drop tablespoons of the mixture on to the surface. Bake the pancakes until golden or for about 3 minutes on each side. Transfer to a wire rack and serve warm or cold with butter or honey.

TREACLE · SCONES · (makes 12)

In the nineteenth century, dark, sticky treacle was used more widely in baking especially in the north of England. Here it gives an attractive caramel flavour to these scones.

4oz (115g) wholewheat flour
4oz (115g) plain flour
Pinch of salt
½ teaspoon (½×5ml) baking
    powder
2oz (55g) butter

1oz (30g) soft brown sugar
2oz (55g) currants
¼pt (150ml) milk
2 tablespoons (2×15ml) black
    treacle
Egg yolk or milk to glaze

Measure the wholewheat flour into a bowl and add the plain flour sieved with the salt and the baking powder. Rub in the butter and stir in the sugar and currants. Mix the milk with the treacle and pour on to the dry ingredients and mix to a soft dough. Turn the dough on to a floured surface and roll out until ½in (10mm) thick. Cut out triangles and place on a floured baking sheet. Brush the tops with egg

Fat Rascals

yolk or milk. Bake in a moderately hot oven (400°F, 200°C; Gas Mark 6) for 12–15 minutes. Serve the scones straight from the oven, cut across and spread with butter or honey.

FAT · RASCALS · *(makes about 12)*

A century ago these fruit scones from Yorkshire were baked on a griddle over a peat fire and were called Turf Cakes. Fat Rascals are at their best eaten while still hot, and spread with butter or cream.

8oz (225g) plain flour	*1 1/2oz (40g) caster sugar*
2 teaspoons (2×5ml) baking powder	*3oz (85g) currants*
1/4 teaspoon (1/4×5ml) salt	*1 large egg*
3oz (85g) lard or butter	*4 tablespoons (4×15ml) milk*

Sieve the flour, baking powder and salt into a bowl. Rub in the lard or butter until the mixture resembles breadcrumbs. Stir in the sugar and currants. Beat the egg with the milk and add sufficient liquid to make a soft dough. Reserve some egg mixture for the glaze. Roll out the dough on a floured surface until 1in (2.5cm) thick. Cut into rounds with a 2in (5cm) plain cutter. Place on a greased baking sheet and brush with the remaining egg mixture. Bake in a hot oven (425°F, 220°C; Gas Mark 7) for 10–15 minutes until well risen and golden brown.

SPLITTERS · *(makes 12)*

This recipe for a fruit scone is from a bundle of yellowing newspaper cuttings of the 1920s given to me by the mother of a friend.

8oz (225g) self-raising flour
1 teaspoon (1×5ml) baking powder
1/4 teaspoon (1/4×5ml) mixed
   ground spice

4oz (115g) lard or butter
1oz (30g) caster sugar
2oz (55g) sultanas
1/4pt (150ml) milk

Sieve the flour, baking powder and spice into a bowl. Rub in the lard or butter and stir in the sugar and sultanas. Mix to a soft dough with the milk. Turn on to a floured board and roll out or pat with your hand until 1in (2.5cm) thick. Use a 2in (5cm) fluted cutter to cut out the scones and place on a floured baking sheet. Bake in a moderately hot oven (400°F, 200°C; Gas Mark 6) for 15–20 minutes. Remove from the oven and as soon as the scones are cool enough to handle split through and spread with clotted cream.

BATEMAN'S · MILL · WHOLEMEAL · FRUIT · SCONES

4oz (115g) wholemeal flour
4oz (115g) self-raising white flour
2oz (55g) light soft brown sugar
2oz (55g) butter
2 teaspoons (2×5ml) baking powder

Pinch of salt
2–4oz (55–115g) mixed dried fruit
Milk to mix
A little cracked wheat if available

Measure the flours and sugar into a mixing bowl. Rub in the butter and stir in the baking powder, salt and dried fruit. Mix in the milk to make a soft dough. Shape the dough into a 6in (15cm) circle and place on a floured baking sheet. Mark the dough into 8 wedges cutting half way through. Brush the top with milk and sprinkle with cracked wheat. Bake in the centre of a hot oven (425°F, 220°C; Gas Mark 7) for about 20 minutes. Transfer the scone ring to a wire rack to cool slightly. Serve warm.

Variation:
Cheese Wholemeal Scones Replace the sugar and dried fruit with 2oz (55g) grated Cheddar and a few chopped herbs, fresh or dried.

BUTTERSCOTCH · CURLS · *(makes 12)*
The spiral of butterscotch filling in these little scones bakes to an attractive golden brown. They can be reheated in a hot oven.

8oz (225g) self-raising flour
1 teaspoon (1×5ml) baking powder
1/4 teaspoon (1/4×5ml) ground
   cinnamon

4oz (115g) butter, softened
4fl oz (100ml) milk
1 egg, beaten
3oz (85g) light muscovado sugar

Sieve the flour, baking powder and cinnamon into a bowl and mix in half the butter. Add the milk and egg and mix to a soft dough. Knead

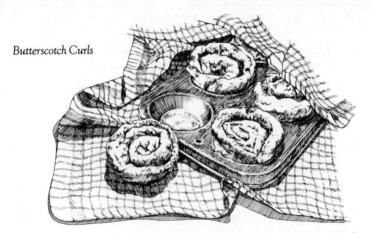

Butterscotch Curls

lightly, then turn the dough on to a floured board and roll out to an oblong 12×8in (30×20cm). Spread the remaining butter over the surface, sprinkle the sugar on top and roll up from the short side. Cut into 12 pieces and place each piece cut side down in greased patty tins. Bake in a moderately hot oven (400°F, 200°C; Gas Mark 7) for 20 minutes. Transfer to a wire rack and either serve warm or cool.

SALLY · LUNN · TEACAKES

Tradition has it that a Sally Lunn living in eighteenth-century Bath gave her name to these yeast cakes which she baked for visitors to the Pump Room. Another possible explanation for their name comes from the French *soleil et lune*, on account of the golden crust of the teacake rising above the paler lower half to resemble the moon eclipsing the sun. Halve and fill with jam and cream while still warm.

*1/2oz (15g) fresh yeast or 1 1/2
  teaspoons (1 1/2 × 5ml) dried
  yeast*
*1 tablespoon (1 × 15ml) caster
  sugar*
*4 tablespoons (4 × 15ml) warm
  water*
2oz (55g) butter
6fl oz (175ml) milk

12oz (350g) strong plain flour
1 teaspoon (1 × 5ml) salt
Grated zest of half a lemon
1 egg, beaten

Glaze:
1 tablespoon (1 × 15ml) milk
*1 tablespoon (1 × 15ml) caster
  sugar*

Cream the fresh yeast with a little of the caster sugar and blend with the water. Alternatively, stir the dried yeast and a little sugar into the water. Set aside in a warm place for 10 minutes until frothy. Melt the butter in the milk over a low heat, cool until lukewarm. Sieve the flour and salt into a bowl and mix in the remaining sugar and the zest of lemon. Add the yeast liquid, milk and egg and beat well with a wooden spoon for 3–4 minutes until the mixture feels elastic. Cover the bowl with a roomy plastic bag and leave in a warm place for about 1 hour or until doubled in size. Beat the dough for 1 minute then divide between 2 well-greased 6in (15cm) round sponge cake tins. Leave in a warm place for 20–30 minutes until the dough is puffy. Bake in a moderately hot oven (400°F, 200°C; Gas Mark 6) for 20 minutes or until golden. Remove from the oven and brush the top of the teacakes with the milk mixed with the sugar. Cool in the tins for 5 minutes then turn out on to a wire rack.

KITTY'S · SPECKLED · BREAD · OR · DOUGH · CAKE

This recipe is a pleasing alternative to the Welsh Bara-brith. In this loaf the fruit is soaked in sweet hot tea until it is swollen and plump. This keeps the teabread moist for some days and gives it an almost yeasty flavour.

12oz (350g) mixed dried fruit
4oz (115g) demerara sugar
1 teacup of milk-less hot tea (strained)

1 egg, beaten
8oz (225g) self-raising flour

Mix the fruit and sugar together in a bowl. Stir in the tea, cover and leave overnight until the fruit has absorbed the liquid. Next day mix in the egg and flour. Turn the mixture into a greased and base-lined 1lb (½kg) loaf tin. Bake in a moderate oven (350°F, 180°C; Gas Mark 4) for 1¼–1½ hours until the loaf is springy in the centre and is starting to shrink from the sides of the tin. Cool in the tin for 5 minutes then turn out on to a wire rack. Serve sliced and spread with butter or honey.

WHIGS · OR · WIGGS

Wiggs date from as far back as the fifteenth century. Until a few years ago they were still baked at Hawkshead village in Cumberland, near William Wordsworth's lodging which now houses a National Trust information centre.

½oz (15g) fresh yeast or 1½
*   teaspoons (1½×5ml) dried*
*   yeast*
6fl oz (175ml) warm milk

12oz (350g) plain flour
4oz (115g) caster sugar
4oz (115g) butter, softened
A few caraway seeds

Blend the fresh yeast with the milk. If using dried yeast first soften it in 3 tablespoons (3×15ml) warm water, then blend with the milk. Set aside in a mixing bowl for 10 minutes in a warm place until frothy. Gradually beat in the flour to make a smooth dough. Work in the sugar, butter and caraway seeds. Cover the bowl with a roomy plastic bag and leave in a warm place for 1–2 hours until doubled in size.

Knock down the dough and knead lightly for 1–2 minutes. Divide in two and make each half into a circle 7–8in (18–20cm) across. Place the circles in buttered sponge cake tins. Mark each circle into 8 wedges and leave in a warm place to rise for 20–30 minutes until puffy. Bake in the centre of a moderately hot oven (400°F, 200°C; Gas Mark 6) for 15 minutes until golden brown. Serve warm or cool on a wire rack. These wiggs reheat well or can be toasted.

WALNUT · AND · BANANA · TEABREAD

Fresh banana makes this teabread soft-textured and moist. This is an ideal loaf for including in a packed lunch or picnic meal.

4oz (115g) butter
4oz (115g) golden or white
*   granulated sugar*
2 large ripe bananas, mashed
1 large egg
3oz (85g) self-raising white flour

1/4 teaspoon (1/4 × 5ml) salt
1/4 teaspoon (1/4 × 5ml)
*   bicarbonate of soda*
4oz (115g) wholewheat flour
2 1/2oz (70g) walnuts, roughly
*   chopped*

Cream the butter with the sugar and the mashed bananas. Beat in the egg and add the white flour sieved with the salt and bicarbonate of soda. Fold in the wholewheat flour and the walnuts. Turn the mixture into a greased and base-lined 1lb (1/2kg) loaf tin. Bake in a moderate oven (350°F, 180°C; Gas Mark 4) for 50–60 minutes until the loaf is firm in the centre and just shrinking from the tin. Cool in the tin for 5 minutes, then turn out on to a wire rack to cool.

HONEY · NUT · LOAF

Honey improves the keeping quality of cakes and loaves due to the moist sweetness it gives them.

4oz (115g) wholemeal flour
4oz (115g) plain flour
1 teaspoon (1 × 5ml) baking
*   powder*
3oz (85g) butter

3oz (85g) mixed nuts, toasted and
*   chopped (ideally almonds,*
*   hazelnuts, brazils and cashews)*
2oz (55g) honey (set or clear)
1/4pt (150ml) milk

Measure the wholemeal flour into a mixing bowl and stir in the plain flour sieved with the baking powder. Rub in the butter and stir in the nuts. Place a small pan on the scales and measure the honey into it. Add the milk and stir over low heat until dissolved. Pour onto the dry ingredients and mix well. Turn the mixture into a greased and lined 1lb (1/2kg) loaf tin and smooth level. Bake in a moderate oven (350°F, 180°C; Gas Mark 4) for 45–50 minutes until the loaf is springy in the centre. Cool in the tin for 5 minutes then transfer to a wire rack to cool.

IRISH · BANNOCK

Irish soda breads made with buttermilk have a fine flavour. If more convenient the buttermilk in the recipe can be replaced with freshly soured cows' milk. This loaf tastes best served warm or toasted.

8oz (225g) wholemeal flour	*1/4pt (150ml) buttermilk*
1/2 teaspoon (1/2 × 5ml)	*1–2 tablespoons (1–2 × 15ml)*
bicarbonate of soda	*warm water*
1 teaspoon (1 × 5ml) salt	

Sieve the flour, bicarbonate of soda and salt into a bowl and then stir in the bran remaining in the sieve. Mix in the buttermilk and add enough warm water to make a soft dough. Shape into a round and place the dough on a lightly floured baking sheet. Mark the top into quarters with a sharp knife. Place a deep cake tin over the loaf. Bake in a hot oven (425°F, 220°C; Gas Mark 7) for 30 minutes. Remove the cake tin and bake the loaf for a further 10 minutes until the crust is brown. Remove from the baking sheet, wrap in a cloth and place in a basket until ready to serve. Alternatively cool on a wire rack.

CRUMPETS · *(makes about 24)*

Metal rings measuring 3–4in (7–10cm) can be bought for cooking crumpets, otherwise use plain cutters of similar size.

1/2oz (15g) fresh yeast or 1 1/2	*1/4pt (150ml) warm water*
teaspoons (1 1/2 × 5ml) dried	*1lb (450g) strong white flour*
yeast	*1/2 teaspoon (1/2 × 5ml) salt*
1 teaspoon (1 × 5ml) sugar	*3/4pt (400ml) warm milk*

Cream the fresh yeast with the sugar and blend with the warm water. Alternatively sprinkle the dried yeast and the sugar into the water in a small bowl. Set aside in a warm place for 10 minutes or until frothy. Sieve the flour and salt into a mixing bowl and mix in the yeast mixture and the milk to make a smooth batter. Set the mixture aside to rise in a warm place for 30–45 minutes. Heat a metal griddle or heavy-based frying pan and grease it lightly. Place the greased crumpet rings on the griddle and when they are hot pour batter into each one until about 1/2in (10mm) deep. Bake over a moderate heat for about 8–10 minutes until the top of the crumpet is set and is full of holes. Remove the rings and turn over the crumpet and bake on the other side for a few minutes until light brown in places. Cool the crumpets on a wire rack. Toast on both sides and serve well buttered.

OLD · ENGLISH · MUFFINS

Toasted muffins, oozing with butter, are a timeless part of a traditional English tea-time.

½oz (15g) fresh yeast or 1½
 teaspoons (1½×5ml) dried
 yeast
1 teaspoon (1×5ml) caster sugar
¼pt (150ml) warm water

1oz (30g) butter
¼pt (150ml) creamy milk
1lb (450g) strong white flour
1 teaspoon (1×5ml) salt
1 egg, beaten

Cream the fresh yeast with the sugar and blend with the warm water. Alternatively, stir the dried yeast and the sugar into the warm water. Set aside in a warm place for 10 minutes until frothy. Melt the butter in the milk over a low heat, then cool to lukewarm. Sieve the flour and salt into a bowl. Add the yeast liquid, the milk and egg and mix to a soft dough. Cover the bowl with a roomy plastic bag and leave in a warm place for 1 hour or until the dough has doubled in size. Turn the dough on to a floured board and knead lightly for 1 minute. Roll out the dough until ½in (10mm) thick and cut out the muffins with a 3in (7.5cm) plain cutter. Leave the muffins, covered, in a warm place for 30–40 minutes or until puffy. Bake the muffins on a hot, lightly greased griddle for 5–6 minutes on each side until golden.

To serve, use a fork to pull the muffins apart all the way round leaving a little in the centre to keep the halves attached. Toast the muffins on both sides then open up and spread with butter.

CHOCOLATE · WAFFLES

Waffles have been made for centuries. In medieval times they were known as wafers and were baked in the same kind of double waffle iron we use today, but with longer handles for heat protection.

3 tablespoons (3×15ml) cocoa
½ teaspoon (½×5ml) ground
 cinnamon
6fl oz (175ml) hot water
2oz (55g) butter, softened
2oz (55g) caster sugar
6oz (175g) plain flour
2 eggs, separated

6fl oz (175ml) milk

For the chocolate sauce:
6oz (175g) plain dessert chocolate
6 tablespoons (6×15ml) black
 coffee
A splash of rum or brandy (optional)
Whipped cream to serve

Blend the cocoa and cinnamon with the water in a mixing bowl. Add the butter, sugar and sieved flour. Stir in the egg yolks and milk. Beat well for 2–3 minutes. Whisk the egg whites until stiff and fold into the mixture. Heat the waffle iron and spoon 1–2 tablespoons (1–2×15ml) of the mixture on to it. Cook for 2–3 minutes until the waffle is crisp outside and is cooked through. Keep the waffles warm, wrapped in a cloth, while you make the sauce. Break the chocolate into pieces and melt with the coffee and rum in a bowl over hot water. Pour the sauce into a small jug and serve with the waffles and, if desired, cream.

· Buns, Pastries · and Tarts

'Here! you go and buy a tart — Mr. Nickleby's man will show you where — and mind you buy a rich one. Pastry,' added Squeers, closing the door on Master Wackford, 'makes his flesh shine a good deal, and parents think that's a healthy sign.'

I don't know about making the flesh shine but the occasional sticky bun or a crisp pastry tart is bound to make most children's, and adults' eyes shine with delight.

Yeast-risen buns are a traditional British food and many of the recipes have changed little over the centuries. Most buns started as regional specialities and gradually became popular further afield. James Boswell wrote in his *London Journal*, 1762–3, 'After the play I came home, ate a Bath cake and a sweet orange, and went comfortably to bed.' At first bakers made buns with the dough left over from making bread. Even today to make a Wiltshire Lardy Cake you need to start with a lump of white bread dough. This is enriched with dried fruit, sugar and plenty of the local Wiltshire fat which is pork lard. The result is a luscious moist, fruity dough cake which is best eaten warm so that the fat seeps through the dough and brings out the yeasty flavour.

In the past buns and yeast cakes were prepared while the main loaves were being baked in the old-fashioned, brick-lined bread ovens still to be seen in many parts of England. As soon as the hot, freshly-baked loaves were ready they were retrieved from the floor of the oven using a peel or long-handled metal paddle which was slid under each loaf to bring it to the small door opening at the front. By now the oven had cooled considerably and the temperature was about right for baking the richer doughs of buns and yeast cakes. These were placed on the oven floor and the metal or wooden door was wedged firmly over the aperture. Sometimes a badly fitting door was itself sealed with a strip of bread dough. After about half an hour the door was removed and the buns were taken out. Some were brushed with a glaze made from sugar dissolved in a little milk or water. They were then popped back in the oven for a few minutes to allow the glaze to dry to the shiny gloss that we find so appetising.

After baking the buns the oven had cooled to the correct temperature for baking the rich pastry tarts. Pastry-making has always been held in high esteem in the English kitchen. And not surprisingly, cooks were keen to display their artistry and skill in this exacting area of baking. In the seventeenth century, pastry tarts became highly decorative. The crust of the tart was cut or pinched into a wide variety of patterns and much ingenuity was displayed in the way the pastry trimmings were cut and rolled, twisted and curved before being arranged in a design on top of the filling.

The fillings themselves were often fruit or preserves. Many housewives enjoyed making a jam tart to show off the extent of their preserves cupboard. Some tarts contained up to twelve different kinds of jam so that the tart looked like a colourful mosaic. Fruit tarts, especially apple, where the decorative lattice or trellis of pastry trimmings was sometimes 'nailed together' with cloves, were very popular. There were also custard tarts made from eggs and milk or cream and flecked with nutmeg and mace; or curd tarts where a soft cream cheese was mixed with eggs and zest of lemon and sometimes a handful of currants. Both kinds have stayed with us until the present day as have the fruit curd tarts made with lemons or oranges and eggs and butter. A table laid for a harvest supper or a country wedding must have been a fine sight in the sixteenth and seventeenth centuries.

In country districts tarts were often covered with a top layer of pastry to make a double-crust tart or pie. This not only made them easier to carry across the fields in a cloth-lined basket to farm workmen for their lunch, it also made the tart into a substantial meal.

CHELSEA · BUNS · (makes 9)

Chelsea buns were an early eighteenth-century speciality of the Bun House in Chelsea where they were baked for local Londoners and the red-uniformed pensioners of the Royal Hospital that overlooks the Thames.

1/2oz (15g) fresh yeast or 11/2
 teaspoons (11/2×5ml) dried
 yeast
1 teaspoon (1×5ml) sugar
4 tablespoons (4×15ml) warm
 water
8oz (225g) strong white flour
1/4 teaspoon (1/4×5ml) salt
1oz (30g) butter
3fl oz (75ml) milk

Filling:
1/2oz (15g) butter, melted
4oz (115g) currants
1oz (30g) dark soft brown sugar
1/2 teaspoon (1/2×5ml) mixed
 spice

Sugar glaze:
1oz (30g) sugar
2 tablespoons (2×15ml) water

Cream the fresh yeast with the sugar and add to the water. Alternatively, sprinkle the dried yeast and the sugar on to the water. Set aside in a warm place for about 10 minutes until frothy. Sieve the flour and salt into a bowl and add the yeast mixture and the butter melted in the milk. Mix well and beat until the dough becomes elastic. Cover the bowl with a roomy plastic bag and leave in a warm place for about 1 hour or until doubled in size. Knock down the dough and turn out on to a floured surface. Knead lightly, then roll out to make an oblong 12×8in (30×20cm). Brush with the melted butter and sprinkle the currants mixed with the sugar and the spice on top. Roll up from the short end and cut into 9 slices. Arrange them in a greased 6in (15cm) square baking tin. Leave in a warm place to prove for about 35 minutes until puffy. Bake in a moderately hot oven (400°F, 200°C; Gas Mark 7) for 25 minutes. Dissolve the sugar in the milk for the glaze, brush the tops of the buns with the glaze and replace in the oven for 3 minutes. Cool in the tin for 3 minutes then transfer the buns to a wire rack to cool.

WILTSHIRE · LARDY · CAKE

Wiltshire is pig country. This means that for baking fine lard is used rather than butter. When my father used to take me to visit my Wiltshire aunts in their low-beamed cottage in Donhead St Mary this sweet, sticky cake, which is also known as Shaley Cake, was always on the tea-table.

1/2oz (15g) fresh yeast or 1 1/2 teaspoons (1 1/2×5ml) dried yeast	3oz (85g) best lard
	3oz (85g) sugar
	3oz (85g) currants
1 teaspoon (1×5ml) sugar	A little mixed spice (optional)
1/4pt (150ml) warm water	A little milk and a little extra sugar to glaze
10oz (285g) strong white flour	
1 teaspoon (1×5ml) salt	

Cream the fresh yeast with the sugar and blend with the water. Alternatively, sprinkle the dried yeast and the sugar into the water. Set the mixture aside in a warm place for 10 minutes until frothy. Sieve the flour and salt into a bowl and mix in the yeast mixture to make a soft dough. Knead for 2 minutes on a floured board. Replace in the bowl and cover with a roomy plastic bag. Leave the dough in a warm place for about 1 hour or until doubled in size. Beat the lard with the sugar and stir in the currants and spice. Knock down the dough, then turn out on to a floured board and roll out into an oblong 12×6in (30× 15cm). Dot two-thirds of the dough with a third of the lard mixture and fold in three as for puff pastry. Re-roll and repeat the larding and folding twice. Finally shape the dough into an 8in (20cm) square and place in a greased 8in (20cm) tin. Leave in a warm place to rise for about 1 hour.

Brush the top of the dough with milk and sprinkle with the extra sugar. Make two diagonal cuts across the top of the cake. Bake in a moderately hot oven (400°F, 200°C; Gas Mark 6) for 30 minutes until golden brown. Cool in the tin for 5 minutes, then transfer to a wire rack. Lardy Cake is best served slightly warm.

DOUGHNUTS · *(makes 10–12)*

Round, jam-filled doughnuts are now made by bakers all over the British Isles. Fifty years ago they were more commonly seen in the south-east of England and the Midlands. Like Lardy Cake these doughnuts originated in Wiltshire where the local pork supplies the fat for deep-frying.

½oz (15g) fresh yeast or 1½	*8oz (225g) plain flour*
teaspoons (1½×5ml) dried	*2oz (55g) butter*
yeast	*1 egg, beaten*
1 teaspoon (1×5ml) sugar	*Raspberry jam*
4 tablespoons (4×15ml) warm	*Oil for deep-frying*
water	*Caster sugar for dredging*

Cream the fresh yeast or stir the dried yeast with the sugar and water and set aside in a warm place for 10 minutes until frothy. Sieve the flour into a bowl and rub in the fat. Add the yeast liquid and egg and mix to a soft dough. Beat the mixture for a few minutes until the dough feels elastic. Cover the bowl with a loose plastic bag and leave in a warm place for about 1 hour until the dough doubles in size. Knead lightly, then turn the dough on to a floured board. Divide into 10–12 pieces and flatten each piece slightly. Place a teaspoon of jam in the centre and press the edges together so that the jam is sealed in. Set the doughnuts aside in a warm place to prove for 30–40 minutes or until puffy. Heat the oil to 374°F (165°C) or until a small cube of bread fries to a golden colour in 1 minute. Deep-fry the doughnuts a few at a time for 4–5 minutes or until cooked right through. Drain on kitchen paper, then roll in caster sugar and eat warm.

HOT · CROSS · BUNS · *(makes 16)*

One a penny, two a penny, hot cross buns,
If you have no daughters give them to your sons,
One a penny, two a penny, hot cross buns.

Most of the spices we know today were brought to Britain by the returning crusaders in the thirteenth century. Cinnamon and nutmeg, cloves and ginger were highly prized. Because of their value and their distinctive flavour they were added to special breads that were baked for religious festivals and feasts. We retain this ancient link in the traditional spiced bun of Easter, baked for Good Friday with its Christian cross on top.

1oz (30g) fresh yeast or 1 tablespoon (1 × 15ml) dried yeast
1 teaspoon (1 × 5ml) sugar
1/4pt (150ml) warm water
1/4pt (150ml) warm milk
1lb (450g) plain white flour or replace half white flour with 100% wholemeal flour
1 teaspoon (1 × 5ml) salt

1 teaspoon (1 × 5ml) mixed ground spice
1 1/2oz (40g) sugar
2oz (55g) butter, melted
2oz (55g) currants
1oz (30g) candied peel, diced
A little pastry for the crosses
A little beaten egg

Sugar glaze:
2oz (55g) sugar
3 tablespoons (3 × 15ml) water

Cream the fresh yeast with the sugar and blend with the water. Alternatively, mix the dried yeast with the sugar and add to the water. Set aside in a warm place for about 10 minutes until frothy. Sieve the flour, salt, ground spice and sugar into a mixing bowl. Add the yeast mixture, milk and butter. Mix well and beat with a wooden spoon until the dough is elastic. Sprinkle the currants and candied peel on top of the dough. Cover the bowl with a roomy plastic bag and leave in a warm place for 1 hour or until the dough has doubled in size.

Knock down gently and knead lightly for 1–2 minutes. Divide the dough into 16 pieces. Shape each into a ball and place, well spaced, on a greased baking sheet. Roll out the pastry thinly and cut into narrow strips. Brush each bun with beaten egg and place a cross of pastry on top of each bun. Leave the buns in a warm place to prove for 30 minutes or until risen and puffy. Bake in a moderately hot oven (400°F, 200°C; Gas Mark 6) for 20 minutes. Dissolve the sugar in the water and brush over the tops of the buns. Replace in the oven for a further 4–5 minutes. Remove and transfer to a wire rack to cool.

BULGARA · BUNS · (makes 24)
Bulgara buns are a variation of the old English Rock Cake.

8oz (225g) plain flour
1/2 teaspoon (1/2 × 5ml) baking powder
3oz (85g) caster sugar
4oz (115g) butter

4oz (115g) sultanas
4oz (115g) stoned dates, chopped
1 large egg, beaten
A little milk
A little granulated sugar

Sieve the flour, baking powder and sugar into a bowl. Add the butter in pieces and rub in with the fingertips until the mixture resembles breadcrumbs. Stir in the sultanas and dates and mix to a dough with the egg. Place teaspoons of the mixture on a greased baking sheet. Brush the tops with milk and sprinkle with sugar. Bake in a moderate oven (350°F, 180°C; Gas Mark 4) for 20–25 minutes until golden. When cool enough to handle move on to a wire rack to cool slightly. These buns are best eaten warm.

ALMOND · AND · ORANGE · SNAILS · *(makes 24)*

Here a rich yeast dough is curled around an orange and almond filling to make snail shapes. The filling is especially good and I find it also goes well in tarts and puff-pastry turnovers.

1oz (30g) fresh yeast or 1 tablespoon (1 × 15ml) dried yeast
3fl oz (75ml) warm water
1 teaspoon (1 × 5ml) sugar
3fl oz (75ml) milk
8oz (225g) butter

12oz (350g) strong white flour
2oz (55g) caster sugar
1 egg, beaten
4oz (115g) ground almonds
4 tablespoons (4 × 15ml) orange-shred marmalade
Beaten egg to glaze

Cream the fresh yeast with the sugar and mix into the water. Alternatively, sprinkle the dried yeast into the water with the sugar. Set aside in a warm place for 10 minutes until frothy. Warm the milk with 2oz (55g) of the butter until melted, then cool slightly. Sieve the flour and sugar into a bowl and add the yeast mixture, the milk and egg. Mix to a soft dough and beat for 1 minute. Cover the bowl with a roomy plastic bag and leave in a warm place for 1 hour or until doubled in size. Knock down the dough then turn on to a floured surface and knead lightly for 2 minutes. Roll out to an oblong measuring 15×8in (37×20cm). Dot two-thirds of the pastry with half of the remaining butter then fold up the bottom third and fold down the top third of the dough as when making puff pastry. Reroll to the same size oblong, and add the remaining butter in the same way. Fold the dough and leave for 15 minutes. Then roll and fold twice more, leave for 15 minutes, then chill, wrapped in plastic, until needed.

Roll out the dough to measure 12×9in (30×23cm). Mix the ground almonds with the marmalade and spread over the dough. Roll up from the short end. Chill thoroughly, then cut into 24 slices. Place, well spaced, on a greased baking sheet and brush with beaten egg. Bake in a moderately hot oven (400°F, 200°C; Gas Mark 6) for 10–15 minutes until golden brown. Cool on the baking sheet for 2–3 minutes, then transfer to a wire rack.

APPLE · DAPPY

Appley Dapply, a little brown mouse,
Goes to the cupboard in somebody's house,
In somebody's cupboard there's everything nice,
Cake, cheese, jam, biscuits,—All charming for mice!
Appley Dapply has little sharp eyes,
And Appley Dapply is *so* fond of pies!

In our family this apple-filled pastry roll is always known as Apple Dappy after Beatrix Potter's charming mouse. Beatrix Potter has left us not only some of the most treasured tales in children's literature but also her house, Hill Top*, and many beautiful acres of Lakeland countryside now owned by the National Trust. To accompany her delightful illustrations of Appley Dapply carrying a plate of tarts Beatrix Potter wrote the verse above.

12oz (350g) prepared shortcrust pastry
1lb (450g) cooking apples
3oz (85g) caster sugar
1/2 teaspoon (1/2 × 5ml) ground cinnamon

1 1/2oz (45g) butter
2 tablespoons (2 × 15ml) golden syrup
2 tablespoons (2 × 15ml) hot water

Roll out the pastry to make an oblong about 14×8in (35×20cm). Peel, core and slice the apples and arrange them evenly over the pastry. Sprinkle with sugar mixed with cinnamon. Dot with the butter cut into small pieces. Roll up the pastry from the short end and place on a buttered oven dish. Mix the syrup and water together and spoon over the pastry. Bake in a moderately hot oven (400°F, 200°C; Gas Mark 6) for 30 minutes. Half-way through the baking spoon the syrup over the pastry. Cool slightly and serve hot or warm, cut in slices.

Variation:
Lemon Apple Dappy Omit the ground cinnamon and mix the sugar with the finely grated zest of 1/2 lemon and a handful of currants.

MOCHA · CREAM · PUFFS · *(makes 12)*

This recipe uses choux pastry. The word 'choux' comes from the French for cabbage and arises from the way a spoonful of the uncooked mixture swells and puffs up in the heat of the oven until it resembles a cabbage. For this reason it is important not to open the oven door until near the end of the cooking time. Mocha cream puffs are very rich — you may prefer to make the miniature versions which are called profiteroles.

3oz (85g) strong white flour
Pinch of salt
¼pt (150ml) boiling water
2oz (55g) butter
2 eggs, beaten

Mocha cream:
2 tablespoons (2 × 15ml) finely
   ground coffee
4 tablespoons (4 × 15ml) milk
4oz (115g) plain dessert chocolate
¾pt (450ml) double cream
2 egg whites
1 tablespoon (1 × 15ml) icing sugar

Sieve the flour and salt on to a piece of paper. Measure the water into a saucepan, add the butter in pieces and stir until melted. Bring to the boil then remove from the heat. Tip the flour and salt into the pan and beat vigorously with a wooden spoon until well mixed. Continue to beat over a moderate heat for a few minutes until the paste forms a ball and leaves the sides of the pan. Remove the pan from the heat and cool slightly. Gradually beat the eggs into the mixture making sure that each addition is well combined. Beat the mixture for 1 minute until smooth and glossy. Place tablespoons in neat heaps on a greased baking sheet allowing plenty of room for them to rise. Bake in a hot oven (425°F, 220°C; Gas Mark 7) for 30–35 minutes until the puffs are well risen and golden brown. Do not undercook or they will be soggy in the middle. Transfer the puffs to a wire rack and immediately make a small vent in the side of each to allow the steam to escape.

To make the cream, heat the coffee with the milk until almost boiling. Set aside to infuse for 10 minutes then strain and cool. Melt the chocolate in a bowl over hot water, then remove and cool slightly. Whisk the cream until stiff then fold in the coffee milk, the melted chocolate and finally the stiffly whisked whites of egg. Spoon the mocha cream into the choux puffs and dust lightly with icing sugar shaken through a sieve.

BANBURY · CAKES · (makes about 15)

A rhyme and a cake have brought fame to Banbury. 'Ride a cock-horse to Banbury Cross, To see what Tommy can buy; A penny white loaf, a penny white cake, And a two-penny apple pie.' Surely the penny white cake must have been a Banbury cake. The filling in the recipe comes from Miss Dorothy Hartley's inspiring *Food in England* (1954) and is the oldest she could trace. It is exceedingly good but may be a little over-spiced for children, so halve the amount given if necessary. In the seventeenth century the pastry was leavened with yeast. Today flaky pastry is used and the cakes are at their best served warm.

13oz (375g) prepared flaky pastry

Filling:
4oz (115g) butter, softened
2 teaspoons (2×5ml) clear honey
4oz (115g) candied lemon peel,
   chopped
8oz (225g) currants

2oz (55g) candied orange peel,
   chopped
2–3 teaspoons (2–3×5ml) ground
   allspice
1/2 teaspoon (1/2×5ml) ground
   cinnamon
1 egg white
A little caster sugar for sprinkling

Roll out the pastry until thin and cut out 4in (10cm) circles. Cream
the butter with the honey and mix in the currants, candied peels and
spices. Place a dessertspoon (1×10ml) of the filling in the centre of
a circle of pastry. Brush the edge with egg white and fold over neatly.
Turn the cake over and flatten slightly. Brush with egg white and
sprinkle with sugar. Place on a greased baking sheet and make a short
slit in the top. Bake in a moderately hot oven (400°F, 200°C; Gas
Mark 6) for 15–20 minutes until the pastry is crisp and golden. When
cool enough to handle transfer to a wire rack to cool.

SUFFOLK · KITCHELS · (makes 15)
Originally Suffolk Kitchels were only baked during the twelve days of
Christmas but nowadays, as with mince pies, they are served at any
time during the winter. Suffolk Kitchels make a delicious alternative
to traditional mince pies.

13oz (375g) prepared puff pastry
2oz (55g) butter, melted
2 tablespoons (2×15ml) light
   muscovado sugar
8oz (225g) currants
2oz (55g) candied orange peel,
   chopped
1oz (30g) candied lemon peel,
   chopped

2oz (55g) ground almonds
1/2 teaspoon (1/2×5ml) ground
   cinnamon
1/2 teaspoon (1/2×5ml) ground
   nutmeg
A little milk to glaze
1 tablespoon (1×15ml) caster
   sugar for sprinkling

Divide the pastry in half. Roll out one piece to fit a greased non-stick
10×7in (25×18cm) baking tin. Mix the butter with the sugar,
currants, candied peels, ground almonds and spices. Spread the mixture over the pastry and cover with the other piece of pastry rolled to
fit. Brush the top of the pastry with milk and sprinkle with caster
sugar. Mark the pastry into 2in (5cm) squares, taking care not to cut
right through. Bake the Kitchels in a hot oven (425°F, 220°C; Gas
Mark 7) for 20–25 minutes. Cool in the tin for 5 minutes, then cut
into squares. Serve warm or cold.

STRAWBERRY · CREAM · HORNS · *(makes 12)*

To make these cream-filled pastries you need a set of cream-horn tins. Of course, other summer fruits can be used to decorate the pastries — raspberries, peaches and blackcurrants are particularly good.

13oz (375g) weight prepared puff pastry
Beaten egg
Caster sugar
Strawberry jam

½pt (300ml) whipped cream
1 tablespoon (1 × 15ml) vanilla-flavoured sugar (see page 00)
About 12 ripe strawberries

Roll out the pastry into an oblong until ⅛in (3mm) thick. Cut strips lengthways 1in (2.5cm) wide. Take a strip of pastry and, starting with the pointed end of the tin, wrap the pastry round the greased mould. Overlap the pastry slightly on the joins. Place on a greased baking sheet, brush with beaten egg and sprinkle with caster sugar. Chill the pastries for 20 minutes. Bake in a hot oven (425°F, 220°C; Gas Mark 7) for 25–30 minutes until the pastry is crisp and golden brown. Cool on the baking sheet for 2–3 minutes, then carefully remove the pastry shapes from the metal cones and place on a wire rack to cool. Spoon a little strawberry jam into each pastry horn and fill with whipped cream sweetened with the vanilla sugar. Place a ripe strawberry in the top of each cream horn and serve.

CRULLERS · *(makes about 30)*

Deep-frying goes back as far as medieval times when a vessel called a *chauffer* fitted to a metal tripod or *blandreth* was used. Crullers are deep-fried pastries from Scotland.

8oz (225g) plain flour
1 teaspoon (1 × 5ml) baking powder
1oz (30g) caster sugar, vanilla-flavoured (see page 00)
¼ teaspoon (¼ × 5ml) ground mace

Grated zest of ½ lemon
2oz (55g) butter
2 eggs
Oil for deep-frying
Vanilla sugar for dredging

Sieve the flour, baking powder, sugar and ground mace into a bowl. Stir in the zest of lemon. Rub in the butter until the mixture resembles breadcrumbs. Mix to a dough with the eggs and turn out on to a floured board. Roll out the dough to ½in (10mm) thickness and cut into crescents or strips which can be twisted. Heat the oil to 374°F (165°C) or until a cube of white bread fries golden in 1 minute. Deep-fry the crullers, three or four at a time, until they are golden brown and cooked right through. Drain well on kitchen paper, then dredge in vanilla sugar and serve warm.

GABLED · TREACLE · TART

'Gabling' dates from medieval times and is the name given to a pastry edge which is cut and folded to look like battlements. Cutting pastry this way not only looks attractive but also makes the crust bake to a delightful crispness which contrasts well with the soft treacle filling in this tart.

For the rich shortcrust pastry:	For the filling:
4oz (125g) plain flour	*4oz (115g) golden syrup*
2 teaspoons (2×5ml) caster sugar	*½oz (15g) butter*
2½oz (70g) butter	*2 tablespoons (2×15ml) double*
1 egg yolk	*cream*
1–2 tablespoons (1–2×15ml) cold	*Grated zest of lemon*
water	*1 egg, beaten*

Sieve the flour and sugar into a bowl and rub in the butter until the mixture resembles breadcrumbs. Mix the egg yolk with half the water and mix into the dry ingredients to make a soft dough. Add more water only if necessary to bind the dough together. Roll out the pastry to fit a greased 8in (20cm) shallow pie-dish or tin. Make sure that the pastry is cut evenly around the edge of the rim of the dish.

Measure the syrup into a small pan and heat gently until warm. Remove from the heat and add the butter, cream, zest of lemon and the egg. Stir until well mixed and pour into the pastry case. With a sharp knife make radial cuts across the pastry rim of the case every ½in (10mm). Fold each alternate 'spoke' into the centre of the tart so that it rests over the filling. Bake the tart in a moderate oven (375°F, 190°C; Gas Mark 5) for 25–30 minutes or until the pastry is crisp and golden and the filling is set.

ALISON · UTTLEY'S · BAKEWELL · TART

Twenty years ago Alison Uttley, the author who has brought so much pleasure to children with her 'Little Grey Rabbit' stories, wrote a cookery book, and it is no less charming than the stories of her animal world. It tells of her childhood in an old farmhouse in Derbyshire. This is her traditional recipe (which I have halved to make a smaller tart) for that county's most famous dish. Alison Uttley writes, 'This was one of our favourite dishes, but it was a rich dish for special occasions only.'

7oz (200g) prepared puff pastry	*4oz (115g) butter, melted*
4–6 tablespoons (4–6×15ml)	*4oz (115g) caster sugar*
raspberry jam	*4oz (115g) ground almonds*
4 egg yolks	*1 egg white*

Yorkshire Secret Cake

Butter an 8in (20cm) shallow pie-dish or tin. On a floured board roll out the pastry to fit the dish. Crimp the edges of the pastry and spread the jam over the base. Mix the egg yolks with the butter, sugar and ground almonds and fold in the lightly whisked egg white. Pour into the pastry case. Bake the tart in a moderate oven (375°F, 190°C; Gas Mark 5) for about 30 minutes until the filling is set and the top is golden brown. Serve cut into wedges while still warm.

Note: The puff pastry can be replaced by shortcrust pastry which I find gives a better contrast to the filling.

YORKSHIRE · SECRET · CAKE

This cake is also known as Double Nodden or Deception Cake. Today we more commonly call two layers of pastry that enclose a filling a pie or a closed tart.

12oz (340g) currants
4oz (115g) candied lemon peel, chopped
2oz (55g) ground almonds
2oz (55g) dark brown sugar

4 tablespoons (4×15ml) dark Jamaica rum
13oz (370g) prepared puff pastry
A little egg yolk to glaze

Mix the currants, candied peel, almonds, sugar and rum together in a bowl and leave, covered, in a warm place for 2–3 hours until the fruit has absorbed all the liquid. Divide the pastry in half and roll out one piece on a floured board to fit an 8in (20cm) greased pie plate or flan tin. Spread the currant mixture on top and cover with the remaining pastry rolled out to fit. Press the edges together well and brush the top with egg yolk. Bake in a hot oven (425°F, 220°C; Gas Mark 7) for 30–35 minutes until the pastry is golden and crisp. Cool in the tin, then cut into wedges.

WINDSOR · TARTLETS · (makes 12)

Eighteenth- and nineteenth-century cooks made far more use of dried fruit than we do today. It's interesting to see how often dried figs appear in the recipes. These tarts are made with dried fruit and nuts.

Pastry:
4oz (115g) plain flour
2oz (55g) butter, softened
1 egg yolk or 1 tablespoon
 (1 × 15ml) milk

Filling:
2oz (55g) dried figs, very finely
 chopped

2oz (55g) ground almonds
2oz (55g) candied orange or lemon
 peel, finely minced
4oz (115g) apricot jam
1 egg, beaten
2 extra tablespoons (2 × 15ml)
 apricot jam
A little caster sugar for sprinkling

Sieve the flour on to a marble slab or into a wide bowl. Add the butter and egg yolk and work the mixture together with the fingertips to make a soft dough. Chill for 15 minutes, then roll out thinly to line 12 greased patty tins. Mix the figs with the ground almonds, candied peel, apricot jam and the egg. Place half a teaspoon of the extra jam in each pastry case and divide the filling between them. Sprinkle the tops of each with caster sugar. Bake in a moderate oven (375°F, 190°C; Gas Mark 5) for 15–20 minutes until the pastry is golden. Transfer the tarts to a wire rack to cool.

CUSTARD · TARTS · *(makes about 12)*

The filling in these classic custard tarts is inspired by Hannah Glasse's baked custard given in *The Art of Cookery made Plain and Easy* (1747). It is simply eggs and cream flecked with nutmeg and cinnamon and lightened with a little flower water. To make less rich tarts replace the cream with milk and add one extra egg.

Rich shortcrust pastry:
4oz (115g) plain flour
1oz (30g) caster sugar
2oz (55g) butter, softened
1 egg yolk

Custard:
1/2pt (300ml) single cream
1oz (30g) caster sugar
2 large eggs, beaten
Pinch of ground nutmeg
Pinch of ground cinnamon
Pinch of ground mace
Rosewater and orange flower water

Sieve the flour and sugar into a bowl. Add the butter and egg yolk and work together with the fingertips to make a soft dough. Chill for 15 minutes, then roll out thinly. Line greased patty tins that are preferably deep rather than shallow. Prick the bases and chill for 10 minutes. Bake in a moderately hot oven (400°F, 200°C; Gas Mark 6) for 10–12 minutes until the pastry is golden. Remove from the oven and reduce the heat to 350°F (180°C; Gas Mark 4). Whisk the cream with the sugar and the eggs. Add the spices and the flower waters according to taste. Spoon the custard into the pastry cases. Bake in the oven for 15–20 minutes until the filling is set. Cool the tarts in the tins, then transfer to a wire rack.

RICHMOND · MAIDS · OF · HONOUR · (makes 18)

Two traditional tales are associated with these small cheesecakes. One says that they were the favourite cakes of Elizabeth I and that the queen sent her ladies-in-waiting out of the palace to collect them from a baker in Richmond. The other story claims that the tarts were so popular with Anne Boleyn when she was maid-of-honour to Catherine of Aragon that Henry VIII named the cakes after her.

7oz (200g) prepared puff or rich shortcrust pastry
6oz (170g) curd cheese
1/4pt (150ml) clotted cream
3 egg yolks
Grated zest of 1/2 lemon
Pinch of ground cinnamon

Pinch of grated nutmeg
3oz (85g) currants
1oz (30g) caster sugar
3 tablespoons (3 × 15ml) brandy
1/2oz (15g) flaked or slivered blanched almonds

Roll out the pastry until very thin and line 18 greased patty tins. Chill the pastry cases while you prepare the filling. Mix the curd cheese with the cream, egg yolks, zest of lemon, spices, currants, sugar and brandy. Divide the filling between the pastry cases and sprinkle a few flaked almonds on top. Bake the tarts in a moderately hot oven (400°F, 200°C; Gas Mark 6) for 20–25 minutes or until well risen and golden brown. Cool in the tins for 5 minutes, then transfer to a wire rack to cool.

LIME · CURD · TARTS · (makes 18)

When in the eighteenth century the Royal Navy replaced the daily issue of lemons (which were given to sailors to prevent scurvy) with cheaper limes, English sailors were dubbed 'Limeys' — a nickname that still survives today. This is a speedy way to make lime curd tarts because the lime filling cooks as the tarts bake. The flavour is particularly fresh and tangy.

For the pastry:
6oz (170g) plain flour
1oz (30g) caster sugar
3oz (85g) butter, softened
1 egg yolk

For the filling:
2 limes
2 large eggs
3oz (85g) caster sugar
2oz (55g) butter, melted

Sieve the flour and sugar on to a cold work surface or into a wide, shallow bowl. Add the butter and egg yolk and use the fingertips to

Queen of Heart Tarts

mix the ingredients together. Slide small handfuls of the mixture along the surface until the dough easily forms a ball. Chill, wrapped, for 15 minutes. Roll the pastry out thinly and cut out circles to line 18 greased patty tins. Prick the bases and chill the tins for 15 minutes while you prepare the filling. Bake the pastry cases blind in a moderately hot oven (400°F, 200°C; Gas Mark 6) for 6–7 minutes until the pastry is set and is starting to change colour. Remove from the oven and reduce the heat to 350°F (180°C; Gas Mark 4).

Wash and dry the limes. Finely grate the zest into a bowl and add the strained juice. Beat in the eggs, sugar and butter. Spoon the filling into the pastry cases and bake for 5 minutes until the filling is set. Cool slightly, then carefully transfer the tarts to a wire rack to cool.

QUEEN · OF · HEART · TARTS · *(makes 15–18 tarts)*

Heart-shaped jam tarts are always popular. I find an almond pastry makes them especially crisp and delicious.

5oz (140g) plain flour	*4oz (115g) butter, softened*
3oz (85g) ground almonds	*1 egg yolk*
1oz (30g) icing sugar	*Raspberry jam*

Sieve the flour, ground almonds and icing sugar into a wide bowl. Add the butter and the egg yolk and work together with the fingertips to make a soft dough. Chill the dough, wrapped, for 20 minutes. Roll out on a floured board and line some greased heart-shaped bun tins. Alternatively, use round fluted tartlet tins and make a small V-shaped wedge at the top with foil to create a heart shape. Spoon the jam into the tarts, taking care not to overfill them. Bake the tarts in a hot oven (400°F, 200°C; Gas Mark 6) for 12–15 minutes until the pastry is golden and crisp. Transfer the tarts to a wire rack to cool.

·Family Cakes·

> There were splits and butter, apple cake, saffron cake and lash-
> ings of cream. By the way, both in Cornwall and London, jam
> was practically unknown to us, and what we saw of it in other
> houses we didn't like. Alice's 'jam every other day' carried no
> fun for me. Now if it had been 'apple cake every other day' I
> should have understood

Thus Mrs M. Vivian Hughes recalls her family holiday tea in the late
nineteenth century in *A London Childhood of the Seventies*. It is when
we come to our own family cakes like apple cake, gingerbread, chocolate cake or cherry loaf that we see the fine tradition of home-baking
that we have inherited.

Here is where we see the effects of our long history as a trading
nation, for this has affected our tastes and gastronomic preferences.
During the reign of Elizabeth I, when her sailors roamed afar, and
travellers like Sir Walter Raleigh brought back new foods, many
exotic flavours became available and were highly valued for the variety
they brought to the diet. Court circles were already accustomed to
some oriental spices and perfumes. Those from the Arab world had
arrived with the returning crusaders in the thirteenth century. By the
fifteenth century ginger and pepper were highly popular, and it was at
this time that gingerbread made with honey, flour and ground ginger,
gilded with the yolk of egg, saffron and dandelion and on occasion
gold leaf itself, was used as a trophy at tournaments. The decoration
marked out with box leaves and cloves sometimes represented the
coats of arms of the jousting knights. This tradition of decorating
gingerbread continued until the late nineteenth century. It can still
be seen on some European gingerbread which is pressed into wooden
moulds to give the surface a pattern before baking. Scottish gingerbread continued to be made in this way longer than in England and
today's gingerbread men and women derive from this tradition of
cakemaking.

Our mercantile past shows not only in our taste for exotic spices
which, being expensive, became a sign of conspicuous consumption
during the inflationary period of Tudor England. We also have a
fondness for a wide range of dried fruit — dates and figs, apricots and

raisins, sultanas and currants — with their sweet, concentrated flavour. The rich, dark fruit cake baked for Christmas and special celebrations has dried fruit as its major ingredient.

During the seventeenth and eighteenth centuries the English housekeeper would buy some imported dried fruit and often enhance it by preserving some of her home-grown fruit like apples, pears and plums and even quinces and apricots. Apple rings threaded on strings were hung outside in the sun in warm weather or otherwise near the fireplace in the kitchen. Dried fruits and even some vegetables like the carrot and parsnip supplied some of the sweetness that is called for in most cake recipes. These ingredients helped to satisfy that liking for sweetness which is common to people of northern Europe and which we developed to a high degree in Elizabethan times. It remains a characteristic of our baking.

Sugar was introduced to Britain by the Romans but for most of our history it has been a luxury. Sugar consumption increased once sugar plantations were established in the West Indies in the late seventeenth century and early eighteenth century. In Britain sugar refining began in 1544 but it was only when Gladstone removed the tax on it in 1874 that consumption soared. Until the nineteenth century many recipes state 'add sugar otherwise honey' in recognition of the scarceness of the commodity. The by-products of refined sugar such as black treacle and brown sugar were always popular in country baking.

Elizabethan account books show an enormous consumption of almonds. These nuts featured in a wide variety of recipes for both sweet and savoury dishes. When finely pounded in a pestle and mortar they were added to the most delicate cakes and puddings. When infused in milk or water the result was an almond milk which was used as a thickener in medieval cooking.

For most of our baking history, white flour has been regarded more highly than the wholemeal variety. Only recently for health reasons has wholemeal flour become more valued. For centuries court circles and the rich ate white, or whitish, bread that was called *manchet* while the poor ate the crusty brown bread of the country.

Until little over one hundred years ago the main raising agent for cakes was either yeast or *barm*, originally an ale barm, or plenty of eggs. But in the middle of the last century a mixture of bicarbonate of soda, tartaric acid and rice flour was produced which has become widely used in today's baking. The new invention was termed baking powder. Yeast is a fine and healthy leavener which is extremely valuable in baking, but it can be tricky to work with and it lengthens the baking process. The huge success of baking powder is due to its reliability and quick effects. However, it is a raising agent to be used with discretion; too much can impair the flavour of cakes and baking.

Butter has always been regarded as a luxury food in Britain. In many parts of the country it has never entirely replaced the lard that has played a major role in country cooking and baking. This fat is usually regarded as in some way inferior, although this did not stop cooks from using it, even covertly. Gwen Raverat tells us in *Period Piece* of her childhood in late Victorian Cambridge:

> . . . My mother had a theory, founded on intuition, that lard was dirty; it was strictly forbidden in our kitchen. But the cook always had plenty of lard — I suppose always called by some other name in the account book — and it was quite safe, for my mother would not have recognised the stuff if she had seen it on the kitchen table.

I was brought up with a similar disdain for lard and it was never purchased by my mother. It is only now that I make my own lard that I am beginning to appreciate it as a cooking ingredient. There is no doubt that it gave much of the old country cooking a distinctive flavour and texture and for some baking, for example Lardy Cake, it is essential. In Devon and Cornwall thick clotted cream replaced butter in much cooking and baking. Devon still has a recipe for rich cakes where clotted cream replaces butter to make a kind of shortbread.

WHOLEWHEAT · APPLE · CAKE

This is an unusual apple cake from the Channel Islands where it is made with wholemeal flour. At its best served warm, this apple cake is good for breakfast or for tea by the fire.

8oz (225g) wholewheat flour	1/2 teaspoon (1/2 × 5ml) grated
8oz (225g) cooking apples	nutmeg
4oz (115g) butter	1/2 teaspoon (1/2 × 5ml) ground
8oz (225g) dark muscovado sugar	cinnamon
2 eggs, beaten	

Measure the flour into a bowl. Peel, core and dice the apples fairly small. Stir the apples into the flour as you prepare them to prevent them from discolouring. Mix well and leave, covered, for 3 hours or overnight. Cream the butter and gradually beat in the sugar and the eggs. Stir the spices into the apple mixture and then mix in the butter mixture until well combined. Turn into a well-greased 11×7in (28×18cm) cake tin. Bake in a slow oven (300°F, 150°C; Gas Mark 2) for 50–60 minutes until the top is crusty and light brown. Cool in the tin for 5 minutes then cut into squares and serve warm with cream.

FLORENCE · WHITE'S · 'REALLY · DELICIOUS' · CHOCOLATE · CAKE

I discovered the recipe for this cake in a newspaper cutting from fifty years ago entitled 'Good Cakes to Cut At'. It is, indeed, really delicious. The layer of caster sugar on top of the cake bakes to a shiny crust and the ground almonds help the cake keep well.

8oz (225g) butter
8oz (225g) caster sugar
6 large eggs, separated
Few drops of vanilla essence

8oz (225g) plain dessert chocolate, grated
3oz (85g) plain flour
4oz (115g) ground almonds

Cream the butter with 6oz (175g) of the sugar until light and fluffy. Gradually beat in the egg yolks and the vanilla essence. Mix the grated chocolate with the flour and ground almonds and stir into the butter mixture. Whisk the egg whites until moderately stiff and fold into the mixture. Turn into a greased and base-lined 8in (20cm) round cake tin, preferably loose bottomed. Dust the remaining caster sugar over the top in an even layer. Bake in a slow oven (325°F, 160°C; Gas Mark 3) for 1½–2 hours until a thin wooden skewer comes out clean from the centre of the cake. Cool in the tin for 5 minutes, then transfer to a wire rack to cool.

SANDCAKE

From Regency times until the end of the seventeenth century it was common to serve a sweet wine with a slice of cake. Madeira cake was served with Madeira wine. Sandcake often accompanied a glass of Old Malmsey or sweet sherry. Today we would more likely serve Sandcake with a sorbet or fruit fool.

8oz (225g) butter
8oz (225g) caster sugar
3 large eggs, separated
A little vanilla essence
4oz (115g) ground rice

4oz (115g) potato flour
4oz (115g) plain flour
1½ teaspoons (1½ × 5ml) baking powder

Cream the butter and sugar until light and fluffy. Beat in the egg yolks with a drop or two of vanilla essence and the ground rice. Mix in the potato flour sieved with the plain flour and the baking powder. Whisk the egg whites until fairly stiff and then fold into the mixture, taking care not to lose too much air. Turn the mixture into a greased and lined 8in (20cm) cake tin lightly buttered and dusted with flour sieved with caster sugar. Bake in a moderate oven (350°F, 180°C; Gas Mark 4) for 1–1¼ hours. Cool in the tin for 5 minutes, then turn out on to a wire rack to cool.

MRS · BEETON'S · COMMON · CAKE

'Suitable for sending Children at School' is how Mrs Beeton describes this cake. This is a yeast-risen cake with little fat so any over is best toasted for tea-time. In the Westcountry this style of cake is known as a dough cake or currant loaf.

1/2oz (15g) fresh yeast or 1 1/2 teaspoons (1 1/2 × 5ml) dried yeast
1/2pt (300ml) warm milk
1lb (450g) plain flour
2oz (55g) butter or clarified dripping, softened

4oz (115g) caster sugar
1 teaspoon (1 × 5ml) caraway seeds
1/2 teaspoon (1/2 × 5ml) ground allspice
8oz (225g) currants

Cream the fresh yeast with a little of the sugar and blend with the milk. Alternatively, soften the dried yeast in 3 tablespoons (3 × 15ml) of warm water and then mix with a little sugar and the milk. Set the yeast liquid aside for 10 minutes in a warm place until frothy. Measure the flour, sugar, butter, spices and currants into a mixing bowl. Add the yeast liquid and mix to a soft dough. Knead the dough lightly for 4–5 minutes until it feels elastic. Shape into a ball and place in a 6–7in (15–18cm) greased cake tin. Tie a collar of buttered paper around the tin protruding 6in (15cm) above the rim. Place the tin in a roomy plastic bag and leave to prove in a warm place for about 1 hour until double in volume. Bake in a slow oven (325°F, 160°C; Gas Mark 3) for 1 1/4–1 1/2 hours. Cool on a wire rack.

WIRELESS · CAKE

Fifty years ago this recipe was broadcast on the wireless. A friend of my mother wrote it down and baked it a lot. I discovered it in her manuscript cookery book.

4oz (115g) butter
4oz (115g) caster sugar
1 1/2 tablespoons (1 1/2 × 15ml) black treacle
2 eggs
8oz (225g) plain flour

2 teaspoons (2 × 5ml) baking powder
2oz (55g) ground almonds
1lb (450g) mixed dried fruit
4oz (115g) candied lemon peel, chopped
1 tablespoon (1 × 15ml) milk

Cream the butter with the sugar and black treacle until light and fluffy. Beat in the eggs one at a time. Fold in the sieved flour and baking powder alternately with the ground almonds mixed with the dried fruit and lemon peel. Mix in the milk if the mixture is very stiff. Turn the mixture into a greased and lined 7in (18cm) round or 6in (15cm) square cake tin. Smooth the top level then make a slight

Wireless Cake

hollow in the centre. Bake in a slow oven (300°F, 150°C; Gas Mark 2) for 1¼–1½ hours. Cool in the tin for 30 minutes, then transfer to a wire rack.

CHERRY · LOAF

To help prevent cherries from sinking to the bottom of a cake, wash off the syrup, dry them and cut into quarters; then roll the cherries in some of the flour in the recipe.

4oz (115g) butter
4oz (115g) caster sugar
2 eggs
4oz (115g) plain flour
½ teaspoon (½ × 5ml) baking powder

2oz (55g) ground almonds
3oz (85g) glacé cherries, quartered
A little granulated sugar for sprinkling

Cream the butter with the sugar until light and fluffy. Beat in the eggs, one at a time. Fold in the flour sieved with the baking powder and then the ground almonds mixed with the glacé cherries. The mixture should be fairly stiff. Turn the mixture into a greased and lined 1lb (½kg) loaf tin. Smooth the top level and sprinkle over some granulated sugar. Bake in a moderate oven (350°F, 180°C; Gas Mark 4) for 50–60 minutes until springy in the middle or a thin wooden skewer comes out clean from the centre. Cool in the tin for 2 minutes, then turn out on to a wire rack.

FRUIT · AND · NUT · UPSIDE-DOWN · CAKE

If you wish to take this cake to a picnic it is best to leave it in the tin and then unmould it when you arrive. Try varying the mixture of fruit and nuts each time you make the cake.

1/2oz (15g) butter
1oz (30g) light soft brown sugar
A selection of fruits, raw, or if
    cooked then well drained, eg
    halved apricots, sliced peaches,
    strawberries, sliced bananas, etc
A selection of blanched and halved
    nuts, eg almonds, walnuts,
    pecans, etc

6oz (170g) butter
6oz (170g) caster sugar
3 eggs
7oz (200g) self-raising flour
1/4 teaspoon (1/4×5ml) vanilla
    essence

Melt the butter and light brown sugar in a small pan. Pour into a greased and lined 8–9in (20–23cm) square tin. Arrange the fruit and nuts on top. Cream the butter with the caster sugar until light and fluffy. Beat in the eggs one at a time. Fold in the sieved flour with the vanilla essence. Spoon the mixture over the fruit taking care not to dislodge it. Smooth the top level. Bake in a moderate oven (350°F, 180°C; Gas Mark 4) for 40–50 minutes until the cake is springy in the centre. Leave in the tin for 5 minutes, then turn out on to a wire rack to cool.

BOILED · FRUIT · CAKE

Boiled fruit cakes, where the dried fruit is first cooked with butter, sugar and water, became very popular during and after the war as a way of making a fruit cake moist enough to keep well yet using a smaller quantity of expensive dried fruits than usual. The apricots and dates give this boiled cake a particularly good flavour.

4oz (115g) butter
4oz (115g) demerara sugar
1/4pt (150ml) water
3oz (85g) dried apricots
3oz (85g) dates
3oz (85g) seedless raisins
3oz (85g) sultanas

3oz (85g) currants
8oz (225g) self-raising flour
1/2 teaspoon (1/2×5ml) mixed
    spice
1 large egg, beaten
1–2 tablespoons (1–2×15ml)
    sherry or orange juice

Measure the butter, sugar and water into a large pan. Add the dried fruit and bring the mixture to the boil. Turn down the heat and simmer the mixture gently for 20 minutes. Remove from the heat and stand the pan in cold water until the mixture thickens but is still soft. Add the flour sieved with the spice and mix in the egg and sherry or orange juice. Turn the mixture into a greased and lined 7in (18cm) cake tin. Bake in a slow oven (325°F, 160°C; Gas Mark 3) for 1–1 1/4 hours or until a thin wooden skewer comes out clean from the centre of the cake. Cool in the tin for 30 minutes, then turn out onto a wire rack.

PINEAPPLE-TOPPED · GINGERBREAD

Medieval gingerbread was always decorated and often gilded with yolk of egg, saffron and even gold-leaf. I've kept to the gold idea by combining sugary glacé pineapple with spicy gingerbread.

4oz (125g) butter
2oz (55g) black treacle
2oz (55g) golden syrup
3oz (85g) molasses sugar or dark
   soft brown sugar
4 tablespoons (4×15ml) milk
1/2 teaspoon (1/2×5ml)
   bicarbonate of soda
2 eggs, beaten
8oz (225g) plain flour.
2 teaspoons (2×5ml) ground
   ginger

1 teaspoon (1×5ml) ground
   cinnamon
1/4 teaspoon (1/4×5ml) grated
   nutmeg

Icing:
4oz (115g) icing sugar
1–2 tablespoons (1–2×15ml)
   pineapple juice
1–2 drops yellow food colouring
   (optional)
2 1/2oz (70g) glacé pineapple, diced

In a large pan melt the butter with the treacle, syrup and sugar over a low heat then cool slightly. Add the milk blended with the bicarbonate of soda, the eggs and flour sieved with the spices. Mix together well, turn into a greased and base-lined 7in (18cm) square cake tin and smooth level. Bake in a slow oven (300°F, 150°C; Gas Mark 2) for 40–50 minutes until the cake is springy in the centre. Do not open the oven door for the first 30 minutes or the cake may sink in the middle. Cool in the tin for 3 minutes, then turn out on to a wire rack.

Mix the sieved icing sugar with sufficient pineapple juice to give a pouring consistency. Colour it pale yellow if you wish and pour over the cake. Decorate with pieces of glacé pineapple and leave the cake in a warm place to set.

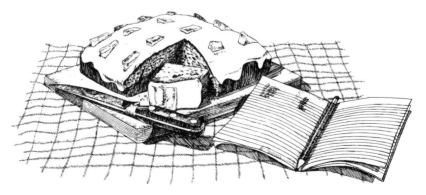

Pineapple-Topped Gingerbread

ORANGE · RAISIN · CAKE

The orange glaze on this cake gives it a lovely taste and helps to keep the cake fresh for up to a week.

5oz (140g) butter
6oz (170g) caster sugar
2 eggs
Zest of 1/2 orange, finely grated
1 ripe banana, mashed
8oz (225g) plain flour
2 teaspoons (2×5ml) bicarbonate
  of soda

6oz (170g) seedless raisins
1/2 teacup buttermilk or sour milk

Glaze:
4oz (115g) caster sugar
Zest of 1/2 orange, finely grated
Juice of 1 orange

Cream the butter with the sugar until light and fluffy. Gradually beat in the eggs with the zest of orange and the banana. Fold in the flour sieved with the bicarbonate of soda alternately with the raisins and milk. Turn into a greased and lined 8in (20cm) square tin and smooth level. Bake in a moderate oven (350°F, 180°C; Gas Mark 4) for 45 minutes.

While the cake is baking, mix the sugar with the zest and juice of the orange and leave in a warm place, stirring until dissolved. Remove the cake from the oven and pour the glaze over the top, spreading it as evenly as possible. Replace the cake in the oven for 5 minutes for the glaze to set. Cool in the tin, then cut into squares.

CARROT · CAKE

In the days when sugar was an expensive ingredient cooks looked for alternatives to use in baking. Honey, fruit and even sweet root vegetables were incorporated into cakes and breads. Carrots and potatoes, pumpkin and marrow all found their way into cakes at some time. The longest survivor seems to be the carrot so that even today new carrot cakes are still being devised. This is a modern carrot cake that is always highly popular.

5oz (140g) butter
7oz (200g) light soft brown sugar
6oz (170g) carrots, finely grated
2 eggs
7oz (200g) self-raising flour
2 teaspoons (2×5ml) baking powder
1 teaspoon (1×5ml) ground
  cinnamon
1/2 teaspoon (2.5ml) ground
  nutmeg

1/2 teaspoon (1/2×5ml) salt
4oz (115g) seedless raisins
2oz (55g) walnuts, chopped
3 tablespoons (3×15ml) milk

Frosting:
6oz (170g) cream cheese
2 teaspoons (2×5ml) lemon juice
1 1/2oz (45g) icing sugar
A little vanilla essence

Melt the butter in a bowl and beat in the sugar, carrots and eggs. Fold in the flour sieved with the baking powder, spices and salt. Add the raisins, walnuts and milk and mix until well combined. Turn the mixture into a greased and lined 9in (23cm) square tin and smooth level. Bake in a moderate oven (350°F, 180°C; Gas Mark 4) for about 1 hour until the cake is springy in the middle and a thin wooden skewer comes out clean. Cool in the tin for 5 minutes, then turn out on to a wire rack.

For the frosting, beat the cream cheese with the lemon juice, sieved icing sugar and the vanilla until light and creamy. Spread over the cake and make a pattern of swirls with the knife. Set aside to dry.

LOUISA'S · HOT · CINNAMON · CAKE

This simple-to-make cake with a crunchy streusel layer on top is very good served hot with thick cream and coffee. This recipe was given to me by Louisa's brother, Guy Czartoryski, because he says he was always delighted to discover it in his tuck box.

12oz (350g) plain flour
2 teaspoons (2×5ml) baking powder
6oz (170g) caster sugar
1 egg
6fl oz (175ml) milk
2fl oz (55ml) corn oil

Streusel layer:
2oz (55g) butter, melted
3oz (85g) brown sugar
1/2 teaspoon (1/2×5ml) ground cinnamon

Sieve the flour and baking powder into a bowl. Add the sugar, egg, milk and oil. Beat together with a wooden spoon until the mixture is smooth. Turn into a greased and lined 7in (18cm) square cake tin. Pour the melted butter over the top and sprinkle the sugar mixed with the ground cinnamon over it. Bake in a moderate oven (350°F, 180°C; Gas Mark 4) for 30–35 minutes. Cool in the tin for 5 minutes, then cut into squares and serve. If serving cold, transfer to a wire rack.

CHOCOLATE · MINT · CAKE

6oz (170g) butter
4oz (115g) caster sugar
6oz (170g) golden syrup
2 large eggs
Vanilla essence
6oz (170g) plain flour
3oz (85g) cocoa
1 teaspoon (1×5ml) bicarbonate of soda
1/4pt (150ml) milk

Icing:
8oz (225g) icing sugar
2oz (55g) butter
3 tablespoons (3×15ml) water
Oil of peppermint
Green food colouring
2oz (55g) plain dessert chocolate, melted

Cream the butter, caster sugar and syrup together until light and fluffy. Gradually beat in the eggs and vanilla essence. Fold in the flour sieved with the cocoa and bicarbonate of soda alternately with the milk. Turn into a greased and lined 8in (20cm) square cake tin and smooth level. Bake in a slow oven (300°F, 150°C; Gas Mark 2) for 1½–1¾ hours. Cool in the tin for 5 minutes, then turn out on to a wire rack.

Sieve the icing sugar into a bowl. Heat the butter with the water and bring to the boil. Remove from the heat and pour on to the icing sugar. Mix in 1 drop of oil of peppermint and tint the icing pale green with a little food colouring. Leave the icing to cool slightly and thicken, then pour over the cake. Spoon the melted chocolate in swirls on top of the green icing and leave in a warm place to set.

MRS · SMITH'S · CHOCOLATE · CAKE

In 1902 Rudyard Kipling bought Batemans*, a fine Jacobean house near Burwash in East Sussex. The adjoining water mill was restored a decade ago by Mr Jim Smith and a team of volunteers. From April until October on Saturday afternoons and Bank Holidays the mill is working and Mrs Edith Smith sells the flour. She kindly gave me her recipe for this wholemeal chocolate cake.

3oz (85g) wholemeal flour
3oz (85g) plain flour
5oz (140g) caster sugar
3oz (85g) butter, softened
1oz (30g) cocoa
1 teaspoon (1×5ml) baking powder
1 teaspoon (1×5ml) bicarbonate of soda
¼ teaspoon (¼×5ml) salt
2 tablespoons (2×15ml) black treacle

2 eggs
Scant ¼pt (150ml) milk

Butter icing:
2½oz (70g) butter
5oz (140g) icing sugar
1–2 tablespoons (1–2×15ml) creamy milk
Vanilla essence
5oz (140g) plain dessert chocolate or caster sugar for decoration

Measure the flours, sugar and butter into a bowl. Add the cocoa sieved with the baking powder, bicarbonate of soda and salt. Mix in the treacle, eggs and milk and beat well for 1–2 minutes. Turn the mixture into a greased and base-lined 7in (18cm) round cake tin. Bake in a slow oven (300°F, 150°C; Gas Mark 2) for about 1 hour until the cake is springy in the centre. Cool in the tin for 5 minutes, then turn out to cool on a wire rack.

When the cake is cold cut across in two layers and sandwich with butter icing made by creaming the butter with the sieved icing sugar, the milk and a little vanilla essence. Melt the chocolate in a bowl over hot water and pour over the top of the cake. Alternatively, dust the top of the cake with a little caster sugar.

PARKIN

Parkin is from the north of England and the oatmeal in the recipe confirms that. This recipe is from Lancashire and tastes excellent.

3oz (85g) plain flour
1 teaspoon (1×5ml) ground ginger
½ teaspoon (½×5ml) mixed spice
½ teaspoon (½×5ml) bicarbonate of soda

8oz (225g) medium oatmeal
4oz (115g) goose or pork dripping
8oz (225g) golden syrup or half syrup and half black treacle
2oz (55g) dark soft brown sugar
3–4 tablespoons (3×15ml) milk

Sieve the flour, ground ginger, mixed spice and bicarbonate of soda into a bowl. Stir in the oatmeal. Melt the dripping with the syrup and sugar over medium heat and stir into the dry ingredients. Pour the mixture into a greased and lined 7in (18cm) square tin. Bake in a slow oven (300°F, 150°C; Gas Mark 2) for 1–1¼ hours. Cool in the tin, then cut into squares.

COFFEE · SQUARES · *(makes 15)*

4oz (115g) butter
4oz (115g) caster sugar
2 eggs
4 teaspoons (4×5ml) instant coffee, liquid or powder
4oz (115g) self-raising flour

Coffee cream:
3oz (85g) butter

1 egg yolk
2½oz (70g) icing sugar
3 teaspoons (3×5ml) instant coffee, liquid or powder
1–2 tablespoons (1–2×15ml) hot water
1 tablespoon (1×15ml) flaked almonds, toasted

Soften the butter and beat with the sugar until light and fluffy. Beat in the eggs, one at a time, with the coffee. Fold in the sieved flour. Turn the mixture into a greased and base-lined 11×7in (28×18cm) cake tin and smooth level. Bake in a slow oven (325°F, 160°C; Gas Mark 3) for 20–25 minutes until golden brown and just starting to shrink from the tin. Cool in the tin for 5 minutes, then turn out on to a wire rack.

Beat the butter with the egg yolk and gradually mix in the sieved icing sugar with the coffee and the hot water until light and fluffy. Spread over the cake and make a neat pattern with the blade of a knife or the prongs of a fork. Sprinkle the almonds on top and cut into squares.

MRS · LEWIS'S · MUESLI · SQUARES · (makes 24)

A reader in Australia sent me this recipe which she says is popular especially with children, and they can make it themselves.

4oz (115g) butter
3oz (85g) honey
Few drops of vanilla essence
6oz (170g) toasted muesli
1 1/2oz (45g) wholemeal flour
1/2 teaspoon (1/2×5ml) ground
   cinnamon

2oz (55g) ground hazelnuts
2oz (55g) grated desiccated coconut
2oz (55g) chopped walnuts
2oz (55g) seedless raisins
4oz (115g) plain dessert chocolate

Melt the butter with the honey in a large saucepan over a low heat. Remove from the heat and stir in the vanilla essence, muesli, flour, cinnamon, hazelnuts, coconut, walnuts and raisins. Mix well, then spoon into a greased 10×7in (25×18cm) non-stick baking tin and smooth level. Bake in a moderate oven (350°F, 180°C; Gas Mark 4) for 20–25 minutes until golden brown. Cool in the tin, but while still warm break the chocolate into pieces and melt in a bowl over hot water. Spread over the biscuit mixture and smooth level. Leave in a cool place until the chocolate has set, then cut into squares.

CHOCOLATE · REFRIGERATOR · CAKE

Many children start to make cakes with this kind of recipe. It is easy to prepare, there is no baking involved and the results are delicious.

5oz (140g) plain dessert chocolate
4oz (115g) butter
1 tablespoon (1×15ml) clear
   honey or golden syrup
1 egg, beaten
4oz (115g) digestive biscuits or
   sponge fingers, broken

2oz (55g) glacé cherries, sliced
1oz (30g) candied angelica,
   chopped
1oz (30g) candied orange peel,
   chopped
1oz (30g) seedless raisins
1oz (30g) flaked almonds

Break the chocolate into pieces and melt with the butter in a bowl over hot water. Stir in the honey and remove from the heat. Add the beaten egg, biscuits, cherries, angelica, orange peel, raisins and flaked almonds. Stir until all the ingredients are well coated with chocolate. Butter a 1lb (1/2kg) non-stick loaf tin and line with Bakewell paper making sure the paper comes up above the rim of the tin. Spoon the mixture into the tin and smooth level. Chill the cake in the refrigerator until set. Wrap the tin in a hot, damp cloth and loosen the paper from the tin with the blade of a knife. Unmould the cake on to a plate. Remove the paper and slice the cake thinly. Wrapped in clingfilm, it stores well in the refrigerator for 1–2 weeks.

QUEEN · MAB'S · OWN · CAKES ·*(makes about 18)*

According to English folklore Queen Mab is a fairy queen who directs our dreams. This recipe comes from a small cookery book written in 1900 by Mrs Louisa S. Tate for children to use and kindly given to me by Anthea Secker when I started to write this book. The cakes are a version of coconut pyramids; however, the addition of the yolk of the egg gives a more delicate flavour.

4oz (115g) desiccated coconut, unsweetened	*3oz (85g) caster sugar*
	1 egg, beaten

Mix the coconut and the sugar together in a bowl. Add the egg and mix with a wooden spoon until the mixture binds together. Take a teaspoonful and form into a ball. Place on a greased baking sheet. Repeat with the rest of the mixture. Bake in a moderate oven (350°F, 180°C; Gas Mark 4) for 15–20 minutes until pale brown. Cool on the baking sheet for 2 minutes, then transfer to a wire rack.

JAPONNAIS · CAKES · *(makes 10–12)*

These little cakes, often known simply as Jap Cakes, were immensely popular earlier this century. They are fun to make but they are highly fragile. If you wish to travel with them it is best to freeze them first so that they can thaw out on the journey.

3 egg whites	*4oz (115g) icing sugar*
6oz (170g) caster sugar	*1 teaspoon (1×5ml) liquid coffee*
3oz (85g) ground almonds	*essence*
2 tablespoons (2×15ml) cornflour	*1–2 tablespoons (1–2×15ml) hot*
	water
For the filling:	*A little icing sugar, sieved*
3oz (85g) butter	

Whisk the egg whites until stiff. Whisk in half the sugar. Sieve the remaining sugar with the ground almonds and cornflour and fold into the meringue. Place spoonfuls of the mixture or pipe spirals using a plain ½in (1.2cm) nozzle to make circles 2in (5cm) across on a baking sheet lined with vegetable parchment. Bake in a slow oven (300°F, 150°C; Gas Mark 2) for 40 minutes. Cool on the baking sheet for 2 minutes, then carefully transfer to a wire rack. Finely crush two of the cakes into crumbs to use as decoration.

Cream the butter with the sieved icing sugar and coffee essence. Gradually beat in the hot water until the icing is fluffy. Sandwich the cakes with the icing and spread a little icing around the sides. Roll the sides in the crumbs and dust the tops with icing sugar. If you wish, place a rosette of any remaining icing in the centre of each cake.

·Special Cakes·

To help us discover how many of the special cakes in this chapter originated it is best to look back to the last century when two particular events happened which had a deep and lasting effect on British home-baking. The first was when Anna, Duchess of Bedford, decided to do something about 'the sinking feeling' that she suffered between mid-day luncheon and formal evening dinner. She devised afternoon tea, not only as a light meal but also as a social event. The craze spread and by 1900 tea-parties, tea-rooms and, in due course, even tea-dances, gave an enormous fillip to teapots, teasets and tea itself. The effect on the food that now traditionally accompanies a cup of tea was immense. Cakes arrived: a wealth of them spilled on to the tea-tables of Victorian England. There was a huge surge of interest in baking new cakes, biscuits and pastries and in devising fresh ideas which were often inspired by the pâtisserie of France, Austria and Germany.

Some of these new recipes were introduced by the famous chefs of the day — Carême, Soyer, Francatelli who were mainly from abroad. And in the fashion of the time they created dishes for their illustrious employers; Carême was the Prince Regent's chef and Francatelli was Queen Victoria's cook. The Victoria Sponge Cake, Queen Cakes and Battenburg Cake all date from this time.

From early in the nineteenth century another event had an even more important effect on domestic cooking. In *Modern Cookery for Private Families* (1845) Eliza Acton wrote, 'The improved construction of the ovens connected with all modern cooking stoves, gives great facility at the present day for *home baking* even in very small establishments.' Until then, if you lived in a house or cottage that lacked a bread oven the only way that you could bake in an oven was to carry your uncooked cake, tarts or buns along the road to the nearest bread baker. Obviously this could be a fairly hazardous operation. As Eliza Acton continues, 'and without this convenience [of an oven] it is impossible for justice to be done to the person who conducts the cookery; and many and great disadvantages attend the sending to a public oven; and it is very discouraging to a servant who has prepared her dishes with nicety and skill, to have them injured by the negligence of other persons.' How distressing it must have been to return home with a cake or gingerbread scorched on one side or dented on the other and possibly uncooked in the middle. Interestingly though, there had been one good result from such widespread use of the public oven. It had led to tremendous diversity in the decoration of, in particular, pies and tarts. This had the advantage that when you came to collect your baked tart or pie you could identify its distinctive pattern of decoration more easily.

It was, however, the arrival of the cast-iron range with its side oven (as in today's Aga and Rayburn) that transformed cooking and baking for the majority of people at this time. Keeping these huge beasts clean and polished with blacking was a dreadful job for the lowliest kitchen maid, and many tears were spilt over these forerunners of today's gleaming kitchen stoves. But for the cooks who used them the possibilities appeared endless to judge by the vast number of cookery books and recipes that were published in the second half of the nineteenth century.

For me, no one can equal the elegant Miss Acton. It was, however, another woman who, borrowing fairly shamelessly from her distinguished predecessor, became more famous and richer, too. Isabella Beeton was persuaded by her husband to produce what became a complete guide to middle-class living in the latter half of the last century. For this was indeed the era of the middle classes. The industrial revolution had led to great wealth for many of its members and they were much taken with the idea of emulating the life styles of the upper classes and the aristocracy. New public schools were founded so that their sons could be educated away from home. Although, of course, their daughters were normally educated at home by a governess, their brothers joined them until old enough to go away to school. Thus, the nursery tea became an established part of the way of life in prosperous households and large houses in Victorian England. Killerton House* in Devon has a fine reconstruction of a late Victorian nursery.

Some enlightened and more modern parents questioned whether they were seeing enough of their children. Mrs C. W. Earle, whose delightful *Pot-Pourri from a Surrey Garden* was a best seller in 1897, wrote, 'In the cases where it is most difficult for a woman to see much of her children — let us say, in the larger houses of the rich in town or country — it is better that children and governess should be turned into the hosts, and that the parents and guests should go to them for tea rather than the usual arrangement of the children being brought into the drawing room.' Clearly at this time, the nursery tea-table was the place to find Eliza Acton's 'Nursery Preserve' and Isabella Beeton's 'Nice Plain Cake for Children'.

It was at about this time, towards the end of the nineteenth century, that the tuck box became part of the life of those children — mainly boys — who went away to school. Children's books of the time and later, contained stories of dormitory feasts and special foods like cakes, buns and tarts that were regarded as treats. The fictional character Billy Bunter who was entitled 'The Owl of the Remove' was portrayed in the schoolboy's weekly The Magnet as an inveterate eater who was constantly munching cream buns washed down with bottles of pop.

Today's tuck boxes are still filled with goodies, some of which are family favourites: perhaps a dark chocolate cake topped with frosting or a moist fruit cake rich with raisins and nuts. If the cakes have to travel far pack them carefully in several layers of paper and place in boxes that are just large enough to hold the cake snugly. Tuck balls of crumpled tissue paper into the corners to stop the cake slipping. I have found that uniced fruit cakes travel quite well by post but it is wise to label the parcel FRAGILE.

When packing a tuck box it is a good idea to provide a variety of cakes and biscuits and some can be quite plain, others can be made with wholewheat flour. Not only is this sensible on grounds of healthy eating, but I find that the food lasts longer. Everyone goes for the sticky, sugary cakes first and leaves the plainer biscuits and cut-and-come-again cakes until later in the week and a kind of natural rationing results. Don't forget to add a pot of jam or honey for spreading on the toast that is always in mass production in schools and gyp rooms. And pack some apples and plain chocolate or some home-made sweets which can revive flagging spirits in no time at all.

FAIRY'S · ORANGE · SPONGE · CAKE

A really light sponge cake with orange buttercream is both tempting and mouth-watering. This one was described 'as light as if made by fairies' by a family of children one summer day. And, fairy-like, the cake disappeared very quickly from the tea-table.

1 large sweet orange	Buttercream:
1 tablespoon (1 × 15ml) caster sugar	3oz (85g) butter
4 eggs	3oz (85g) caster sugar
4oz (115g) caster sugar	
4oz (115g) plain flour	

Wash and dry the orange and remove one long strip of peel. Cut into long narrow slivers and blanch in boiling water for 3 minutes. Drain and toss in caster sugar. Set aside until needed to decorate the cake.

Whisk the eggs with the caster sugar and a teaspoon of finely grated zest of orange until light and foamy. Use an electric mixer or set the

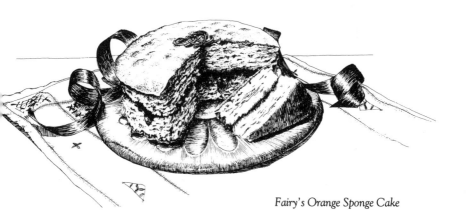

Fairy's Orange Sponge Cake

bowl over hot water and whisk until a trail can be left across the surface of the mixture. Sieve a layer of flour on to the mixture and fold in by hand using the whisk or a metal spoon in a figure of eight. Repeat until all the flour has been incorporated. Divide the mixture between two greased and base-lined 7½in (19cm) tins and spread level. Bake in a moderate oven (350°F, 180°C; Gas Mark 4) for 20–25 minutes until the cakes are golden and are just beginning to shrink from the sides of the tin. Cool in the tin for 2 minutes, then turn out on to a wire rack.

For the filling, cream the butter with the sugar until light and fluffy. Slightly warm the strained juice of the orange with the remaining finely grated zest of orange. Gradually add the orange juice to the butter mixture, beating in each addition well. The buttercream should be really smooth. Sandwich the cakes with half the buttercream and spread the remainder on top. Make a circular pattern with the prongs of a fork and arrange the slivers of sugared orange peel in the centre.

ANGEL · CAKE

This delightfully light, white cake is excellent served plain with custards or ices or dressed up with a rich Orange and Lemon Cream.

3oz (85g) plain flour	1 teaspoon (1×5ml) cream of tartar
½oz (15g) cornflour	1 teaspoon (1×5ml) vanilla essence
6oz (170g) caster sugar	½ teaspoon (½×5ml) almond
6 large egg whites	essence

Sieve the flour with the cornflour and 4oz (115g) of the sugar on to a sheet of paper. Whisk the egg whites with the cream of tartar in a wide bowl until stiff and fluffy but still a little moist. (Do not whisk until dry.) Sprinkle the rest of the sugar over the meringue and whisk in. Fold in the vanilla and almond essence. Sieve the flour mixture into the meringue, folding it in at the same time. Spoon the mixture into an ungreased 10in (25cm) ring tin and smooth level. Bake in a slow oven (325°F, 160°C; Gas Mark 3) for 45–55 minutes. Cool in the tin for 10 minutes then carefully loosen the cake with a flexible knife and turn on to a wire rack to cool.

Orange and Lemon Cream:

1 orange	2oz (55g) caster sugar
1/2 lemon	1/2pt (300ml) double cream
1 egg	

Wash and dry the orange and remove one long strip of zest without the pith. Cut into very fine shreds. Blanch in boiling water for 2 minutes then drain and cool. Grate the remainder of the zest of orange into a bowl and add the strained juice. Add the finely grated zest and juice of the lemon. Whisk in the egg and sugar and stir continuously over boiling water until the mixture thickens. Remove from the heat and allow to cool. Whisk the cream until stiff, then fold in the orange and lemon custard. Spread the mixture thickly over the cake in a swirling pattern. Decorate with the shreds of orange zest arranged on top.

BATTENBURG · CAKE

This cake was named after Prince Henry of Battenburg. It is distinguished by the checkerboard of pink and yellow squares and its wrapping of marzipan.

6oz (170g) butter	Pink food colouring
6oz (170g) caster sugar	Apricot jam
3 eggs	12oz (350g) marzipan
6oz (170g) self-raising flour	A little icing sugar
1/4 teaspoon (1/4×5ml) vanilla essence	

Cream the butter with the caster sugar and beat until light and fluffy. Gradually beat in the eggs and fold in the sieved flour. Mix the vanilla essence into half of the mixture and spoon into a greased and base-lined 11×7in (28×18cm) Swiss-roll tin divided across with a folded piece of Bakewell paper. Add a little pink food colouring to the remaining mixture and spoon into the other half of the tin. Smooth the mixture level. Bake in a moderate oven (375°F, 190°C; Gas Mark 5) for 35–40 minutes until the cake is springy in the centre. Cool in the tin for 2 minutes, then turn out on to a wire rack and peel off the paper to separate the two cakes. When the cakes are cold trim them to make them of equal size and cut both cakes in half lengthways.

Spread apricot jam over the surface of each strip of cake and sandwich them together to give alternating squares.

Roll out the marzipan on a board lightly dusted with icing sugar to make a rectangle about 16×8in (40×20cm) or large enough to wrap round the cake excluding the ends. Place the cake on the marzipan and wrap round pressing the join together. Trim the ends if necessary. Crimp the upper corners with your finger and thumb as for a pie crust and lightly mark a lattice pattern on the top with the blade of a knife. Wrap the cake in greaseproof paper or store in a lidded plastic box overnight before cutting.

RUSSIAN · CAKE

This cake which seems almost to have disappeared is worth reviving.

4oz (115g) butter
4oz (115g) caster sugar
2 eggs, beaten
4oz (115g) self-raising flour
Few drops pink food colouring
1 tablespoon (1×15ml) cocoa
2 tablespoons (2×15ml) hot water
8oz (225g) marzipan
4 tablespoons (4×15ml) raspberry
  jam, sieved

2oz (55g) caster sugar
6 tablespoons (6×15ml) water
1–2 tablespoons (1–2×15ml)
  white rum or kirsch

Icing:
6oz (170g) icing sugar
Hot water
Pink food colouring
1 teaspoon (1×5ml) cocoa

Cream the butter with the caster sugar until light and fluffy. Gradually beat in the eggs. Fold in the sieved flour. Spoon one third of the mixture into a greased and lined 7×7in (18×18cm) tin. Add a few drops of pink colouring to half the remaining mixture and spoon into the cake tin. Blend the cocoa with the water and mix in to the remaining cake mixture. Spoon into the cake tin. Bake in a moderate oven (375°F, 190°C; Gas Mark 5) for 25–30 minutes. Cool in the tin for 2 minutes, then turn out on to a wire rack.

Line the base and sides of a 1lb (½kg) loaf tin with Bakewell paper. Halve the marzipan and roll out one piece to fit the bottom of the cake tin. Cut the cake into ¼in (5mm) strips and brush jam on one side of each piece. Arrange the strips in random fashion on top of the marzipan. Dissolve the sugar in the water, bring to the boil and simmer for 5 minutes. Cool, then mix in the rum or kirsch. Pour over the cake. Cover with the remaining marzipan rolled out to fit. Place a piece of foil-covered cardboard on top of the cake and weight it lightly. Chill overnight.

Unmould and ice the top and sides of the cake with pink glacé icing made by mixing the sieved icing sugar with sufficient hot water to give

a pouring consistency and tinting it pale pink with food colouring.
Reserve a small amount of pink icing and beat in the cocoa. Pipe the
chocolate icing in fine lines on top and then, before it sets, draw a fine
skewer or needle across the lines first in one direction and then in the
other to give a feathered effect. Leave the cake in a warm place until
the icing is set. Serve in very thin slices.

JELLY-BABY · JELLY · ROLL

The alternative name for a Swiss-roll is a jelly roll. This is the version
that I made for some young friends. Vanilla-flavoured sugar is made
by burying a vanilla pod, broken in two, in a jar of caster sugar.

2 large eggs
2oz (55g) vanilla-flavoured caster
  sugar
2oz (55g) plain flour
Pinch of baking powder
A little extra caster sugar

6 tablespoons (6×15ml) raspberry
  or redcurrant jelly
1 tablespoon (1×15ml) small
  diamond-shaped jelly sweets
4oz (115g) jelly babies

Whisk the eggs with the caster sugar until light and foamy and the
whisk leaves a trail across the mixture. For speed use an electric beater
or place the bowl over simmering water while you whisk. Fold in the
flour sieved with the baking powder. Turn the mixture into a greased
and base-lined Swiss-roll tin 12×8in (30×20cm) and spread level.
Bake in a moderately hot oven (400°F, 200°C; Gas Mark 6) for 12–15
minutes until springy in the middle. Turn the cake out on to a sheet
of greaseproof paper dusted with caster sugar and peel off the paper.
Trim the crusty edges from the cake and spread evenly with the jelly.
Sprinkle the jelly sweets over and roll up starting from the short end.
Place on a wire rack with the end tucked underneath. When cold
arrange a row of jelly babies along the top of the roll.

CHOCOLATE · SWISS · ROLL ·
WITH · HAZELNUT · CREAM

3 large eggs
3½oz (100g) caster sugar
2oz (55g) self-raising flour
1oz (30g) cocoa
A little extra caster sugar

Filling:
2oz (55g) hazelnuts, toasted
½pt (300ml) double cream

1 tablespoon (1 × 15ml) caster
  sugar
1oz (30g) plain dessert chocolate,
  grated

Icing:
3oz (85g) plain dessert chocolate
1 tablespoon (1 × 15ml) double
  cream

Whisk the eggs with the sugar in a mixing bowl set over simmering water until light and foamy and the whisk leaves a trail across the mixture. Alternatively use an electric mixer. Gradually fold in the flour sieved with the cocoa until well combined, but take care not to lose air from the mixture. Pour into a greased and lined (the base and ends only) Swiss roll tin 13×9in (32×23cm). Bake in a moderately hot oven (400°F, 200°C; Gas Mark 6) for 12–15 minutes until the cake is shrinking a little from the sides of the tin and the centre is springy. Turn out the cake on to a teacloth lightly sprinkled with caster sugar. Trim off the crisp edges of the cake and roll up the cake from the short side with the cloth folded inside taking the place of the filling. Leave on a wire rack until nearly cold.

Slice a few of the hazelnuts and set aside for the decoration. Finely chop the remainder. Whisk the cream until stiff, fold in the sugar, the chopped hazelnuts and the grated chocolate. Unroll the Swiss roll and spread with the cream, then re-roll. Melt the chocolate with the cream in a bowl over hot water. Spoon over the Swiss roll and sprinkle with the flaked hazelnuts. Chill until ready to serve. The flavour of this cake improves if made a day ahead.

RASPBERRY · CREAM · BASKETS · (makes 12–15)

These cakes are a variation of Butterfly Cakes. They look rather attractive with their angelica handles and rosettes of pale pink cream.

4oz (115g) butter
4oz (115g) caster sugar
2 eggs
Pink food colouring
5oz (140g) self-raising flour

Raspberry cream:
4oz (115g) fresh raspberries,
  puréed
2oz (55g) butter
2oz (55g) caster sugar
1–2 tablespoons (1–2 × 15ml)
  raspberry jam
2–3oz (55–85g) candied angelica

Cream the butter with the sugar until light and fluffy. Gradually beat in the eggs with a little pink food colouring and 1–2 teaspoons (1–2 ×5ml) of the puréed raspberries. Fold in the sieved flour. Place dessertspoons of the mixture into 12–15 greased patty tins. Bake in a moderate oven (375°F, 190°C; Gas Mark 5) for 15–20 minutes until well risen and golden. When cool enough to handle transfer the cakes to a wire rack. Make the raspberry cream while the cakes cool.

Cream the butter with the sugar until light and fluffy. Warm the purée gently, then gradually beat it into the butter and sugar mixture until light and fluffy. Spoon the cream into a forcing bag fitted with a star nozzle. Slice the top from each cake to make a lid for the basket. Place a little raspberry jam on the cut surface and pipe some rosettes of cream on top. Replace the top of the cake, at an angle if it looks prettier. Cut a narrow strip of angelica and curve it over the cake pressing it down on each side to make a handle. Make a few angelica leaves cut in diamond shapes and arrange two or three on each cake tucked in between the rosettes.

ANIMAL · MERINGUES

The light-white meringue made from egg whites and sugar dates from the early eighteenth century and its invention is attributed to a Swiss pastrycook called Gasparini. Meringues soon became a huge success, especially with the monarchy. Although they have only two ingredients, preparing the fluffy white mixture was fairly hard work up until this century. First of all a lump of sugar was cut from a much larger mound of sugar using sugar shears or scissors. This lump was then crushed, a little at a time, in a pestle and mortar to make a fine powdered sugar. The egg whites were whisked by hand and slowly and gently the sugar was folded in. The meringues were shaped with two spoons because the forcing bag was not devised until the early nineteenth century. They were then cooked, or more correctly dried, in a bread oven that had cooled adequately after the day's baking to the temperature required to keep the meringue beautifully white.

These meringue animals are very popular at children's parties and if you make some in miniature they can be used as a cake decoration. For example, an Easter cake made from the Angel Cake recipe (see page 47) can be decorated with tiny meringue rabbits. It is also quite easy to make meringue snails, mice, hedgehogs and swans.

4 egg whites
8oz (225g) caster sugar
Few almonds, slivered

Pink and green food colouring
1 or 2 sticks of liquorice

Whisk the egg whites until stiff. Gradually whisk in the sugar, a tablespoon at a time. Prepare the almonds. Set some aside to use plain and tint half the remainder pink by mixing a little pink food colouring with a drop or two of water. Toss the almonds in the mixture and then drain on kitchen paper. Repeat with green food colouring for the rest. Pipe all the meringues on to baking sheets lined with non-stick baking paper.

Meringue mice

Spoon some meringue mixture into a forcing bag fitted with a ¾in (2cm) plain nozzle. To make the oval shape of the mouse start by piping a fat blob, then drag the forcing bag away from the blob and towards you to end the meringue in a point for the nose. Add two pink almond slivers for eyes and a liquorice tail.

Meringue rabbits

Follow the instructions for meringue mice, then add a blob for the head at the pointed end and another smaller blob at the blunt end for a tail. Add pink almond ears and green almond eyes.

Meringue swans

Spoon some meringue mixture into a forcing bag fitted with a plain ½in (10mm) nozzle. Pipe a small S shape curved to represent the swan's neck. To do this, start with the bottom of the neck near the body then pipe up into an S shape and finish by pulling the forcing bag away to form a point for the beak. Now pipe the body in an oval blob that overlaps the blunt end of the swan's neck. If you are very adept you may be able to pipe a folded wing on to the body. Add an almond eye.

Meringue snails

Spoon some meringue mixture into a forcing bag fitted with a plain ½in (10mm) nozzle. Start with the head of the snail by piping a round blob, then pull the bag away to a point. Now pipe the shell in a spiral with two or three turns that covers the pointed neck end of the head. Make two eyes with green almonds and two horns with liquorice.

Meringue hedgehogs

Spoon some meringue mixture into a forcing bag fitted with a 10- or 12-pointed star nozzle. Start with the tail end of the hedgehog by piping a generous blob, then pull the bag away towards you to drag the blob to a pointed nose. Stick natural-coloured slivered almonds over the body to represent spines and add liquorice eyes.

Bake the meringues in a cool oven (200°F, 100°C; Gas Mark ¼) for 1–1½ hours depending on the size of the animals. Turn off the oven and leave the meringues to cool in the oven for 1 hour. Transfer to a wire rack, then pack the meringues between layers of tissue paper in an air-tight plastic box until needed.

RAINBOW · CAKE

Rainbows have a magical quality, particularly for children. Where do they come from? And where do they go? Is there really a pot of gold at the end of the rainbow? I suppose the ideal time of year to make this cake is in the spring, perhaps April, when the sun is strong enough to shine through a shower to make a lovely coloured arc in the sky. If you've forgotten the colours in a rainbow they are, in order, as follows: red, orange, yellow, green, blue, indigo, violet. You only need red, yellow and blue food colours to mix them all.

6oz (170g) butter, softened
6oz (170g) caster sugar
3 eggs
7oz (200g) self-raising flour
1½ teaspoons (1½ × 5ml) baking powder
Red, yellow and blue food colours

Icing:
6oz (170g) icing sugar
Hot water
A few rainbow-coloured sweets (eg Smarties)

Measure the butter, sugar, eggs and flour sieved with the baking powder into a mixing bowl or a food processor. Mix everything together until really smooth. Divide the mixture into 7 portions each a little smaller than the one before. Colour them according to the rainbow starting with red for the largest amount. Spoon the mixture into a greased 7–8in (18–20cm) ring tin and spread level. Continue with layers of the other rainbow colours in sequence. For orange mix red and yellow, for green mix blue and yellow, for indigo mix blue and violet and violet is made by mixing blue and red together. Smooth the top of the mixture level. Bake in a moderate oven (375°F, 190°C; Gas Mark 5) for 45 minutes. Cool in the tin for 4 minutes, then turn out on to a wire rack to cool.

Mix the sieved icing sugar with sufficient hot water to give a pouring consistency. Add 1 or 2 drops of blue colouring and 1 drop of green colouring to make the icing sky-blue. Pour over the cake and decorate with a few rainbow-coloured sweets. Cut the cake in pieces across so that each piece has all the colours of the rainbow in it.

CHOCOLATE · CRACKER · CAKE

This is a delicious uncooked chocolate cake simple enough for children to make — the work is in the chopping, supervised of course! It makes a good Christmas present, wrapped like a cracker.

7oz (200g) plain dessert chocolate
1 tablespoon (1 × 15ml) rum or
brandy
4oz (115g) unsalted butter
1 egg yolk
2oz (55g) dried apricots, chopped
2oz (55g) dried figs, chopped
2oz (55g) dried dates, chopped
2oz (55g) glacé pineapple, chopped

2oz (55g) glacé cherries, sliced
2oz (55g) candied orange peel,
chopped
2oz (55g) toasted hazelnuts,
chopped
2oz (55g) toasted almonds, chopped
1oz (30g) glacé ginger, chopped
2oz (55g) chocolate flakes or
vermicelli

Break the chocolate into pieces and melt with the rum or brandy in a bowl over simmering water. Cream the butter with the egg yolk until light and fluffy. Gradually beat in the slightly cooled chocolate. Mix in all the dried fruits and nuts until well combined. Spoon the mixture on to a sheet of Bakewell paper and form into the shape of a sausage. Wrap in the paper and chill until almost set. Reshape by rolling again if necessary and roll in the chocolate flakes or vermicelli. Chill until firm. Wrap in fresh paper and pretty ribbons and set aside in a cold place until ready to eat. Serve in thin slices, as it is rich.

CHOCOLATE · HEDGEHOG · CAKE

For centuries the hedgehog has been a favourite shape for puddings and cakes. The 'spines' are usually made of split almonds or candied fruit and then a custard, glaze or icing is spooned on top to coat the whole hedgehog. Children, in particular, love this decorative effect.

4oz (115g) butter
4oz (115g) caster sugar
5oz (140g) plain dessert chocolate,
melted
6 eggs, separated
4oz (115g) ground almonds
2oz (55g) fine white breadcrumbs
3oz (85g) sieved flour

Decoration:
2oz (55g) blanched almonds,
slivered
5oz (140g) plain dessert chocolate
1/2oz (15g) butter
1 egg yolk
2 currants or circles of liquorice

Cream the butter with the caster sugar until light and fluffy. Beat in the melted chocolate with the egg yolks. Fold in the ground almonds and breadcrumbs mixed with the sieved flour. Finally fold in the stiffly whisked egg whites. Turn the mixture into a greased and lined 2lb (1kg) loaf tin. Bake the cake in a moderate oven (350°F, 180°C; Gas

Mark 4) for 50–60 minutes until the cake is springy in the centre. Turn out on to a wire rack to cool. Trim the cake with a knife to make it look reasonably like a hedgehog. Press the almonds in all over to resemble spines but leave an area around the nose free of spines. Melt the chocolate in a bowl over hot water and beat in the butter and egg yolk. Spoon the chocolate over the cake until completely coated. Press in the currants to make eyes and set the cake aside until the icing has dried.

WALNUT · LAYER · CAKE · WITH · WHITE · FROSTING

Many of us share childhood memories of this walnut cake with its snow-white icing which was one of the most popular cakes in Fuller's pink and white teashops until they disappeared.

4 eggs	Frosting:
4oz (115g) caster sugar	2 egg whites
4oz (115g) plain flour	12oz (340g) caster sugar
1 teaspoon (1×5ml) baking powder	1/4 teaspoon (1/4×5ml) cream of tartar
5oz (140g) walnuts, finely chopped	1/4 teaspoon (1/4×5ml) vanilla essence
1 1/2oz (45g) butter, melted	4 tablespoons (4×15ml) hot water
1/4 teaspoon (1/4×5ml) vanilla essence	8 walnut halves

Whisk the eggs and sugar using an electric mixer or in a mixing bowl set over hot water until the beater leaves a trail across the surface of the mixture. Fold in the flour sieved with the baking powder alternately with the walnuts, butter and vanilla essence, taking care not to drive too much air out of the mixture. Turn the mixture into three greased and base-lined 7in (18cm) tins. Smooth the mixture level. Bake in a moderate oven (350°F, 180°C; Gas Mark 4) for 25 minutes or until the cakes are just starting to shrink from the tin. Cool in the tins for 2 minutes, then turn out on to a wire rack.

To make the frosting, whisk the egg whites with the sugar, cream of tartar and hot water in a large mixing bowl set over simmering water. This usually takes about 7 minutes and so the frosting is also called Seven Minute Frosting. When the frosting is ready the meringue is thick enough to stand up in peaks. Remove the bowl from over the water, stand it on a cold damp cloth and continue to whisk until the frosting is cool. Whisk in the vanilla essence. Sandwich the cakes with the frosting and spread the rest in a thick layer over the sides and top of the cake. Decorate the top with the walnuts and leave the cake in a warm place for 1–2 hours until the frosting is set.

CHRISTMAS · RING · CAKE

The circle and the ring are ancient symbols for festivities, possibly based on the sun and the moon. We still tie round garlands of greenery on our doors at Christmas. A fruit cake in this shape looks especially festive. Instead of the usual marzipan and royal-icing decoration, this cake is topped with a medley of glacé fruits and nuts covered with a shiny fruit glaze. Tie a red ribbon around the cake and finish with a huge bow.

8oz (225g) butter
8oz (225g) light muscovado sugar
4 eggs, beaten
9oz (250g) plain flour
1 teaspoon (1×5ml) mixed spice
1/2 teaspoon (1/2×5ml) ground
  cinnamon
1/2 teaspoon (1/2×5ml) ground
  nutmeg
12oz (350g) seedless raisins
6oz (170g) glacé pineapple,
  chopped
6oz (170g) best dried apricots,
  chopped
6oz (170g) glacé cherries, sliced

6oz (170g) pecan nuts or half
  almonds and half hazelnuts
4 tablespoons (4×15ml) dark
  Jamaican rum

Decoration:
4oz (115g) glacé cherries in green,
  red and yellow
2oz (55g) blanched almonds,
  toasted
2oz (55g) pecan nuts, halved
2oz (55g) glacé pineapple, cut in
  neat pieces
2 tablespoons (2×15ml) apricot
  jam, warmed and sieved

Cream the butter with the sugar until light and fluffy. Gradually beat in the eggs, adding a little flour if the mixture starts to curdle. Mix in the flour sieved with the spices and stir in the raisins, pineapple, apricots, cherries, and nuts and mix well. Turn the mixture into a greased 8–9in (20–23cm) ring tin. Smooth the mixture level and tie a double layer of brown paper around the outside of the tin that projects about 3–4in (7.5–10cm) above the cake tin. Bake the cake in a slow oven (300°F, 150°C; Gas Mark 2) for 1½ hours. Reduce the heat to 275°F (130°C; Gas Mark 1) for a further 1–2 hours. The cake is cooked when a thin wooden skewer comes out clean from the deepest part of the cake. Cool the cake in the tin, then turn out on to a wire rack. Make several holes in the base of the cake and pour in the rum. Wrap the cake in double-thickness greaseproof paper and store for 3–4 weeks in an air-tight plastic box in a very cold place.

To decorate the cake, brush the top with apricot jam. Arrange the cherries, nuts and pineapple on top and brush lightly with the remaining jam. Leave the cake in a warm dry place overnight for the glaze to set.

HUNGARIAN · GYPSY · CAKE

This is a cake from the Twenties, discovered in a newspaper article under the heading 'Home cake-making still a flourishing industry'. The cake is best served warm topped with hot coffee and accompanied by soured cream.

11oz (310g) self-raising flour
1/2 teaspoon (1/2×5ml) mixed spice
4oz (115g) butter
3oz (85g) caster sugar
6oz (170g) sultanas
2oz (55g) preserved stem ginger, chopped

4oz (115g) black treacle
3 eggs, beaten
1 after-dinner cup strong hot black coffee
1/2pt (300ml) soured cream

Sieve the flour and spice into a bowl and rub in the butter. Stir in the sugar, sultanas and ginger. Heat the black treacle in a pan. Remove from the heat and beat in the eggs. Mix into the dry ingredients and beat for 1–2 minutes. Turn the mixture into a lined 8in (20cm) square cake tin and smooth the top level. Bake in a moderate oven (350°F, 180°C; Gas Mark 4) for 50–60 minutes until the centre is springy and the cake is just shrinking from the tin. Cool in the tin for 3 minutes, then turn out on to a flat wooden or china platter and swirl the coffee over the top. Serve warm, cut into squares with soured cream.

AUNTIE · CAREY'S · FRUIT · CAKE

This well-spiced fruit cake makes a good birthday or celebration cake. The recipe comes from my mother's manuscript book and the cake was regularly made by her aunt at the beginning of this century. Auntie Carey used to store the cake, wrapped in butter muslin, in a wooden drawer of the dresser. Incidentally the original cake is twice as big — Auntie Carey had a large family. If you can keep the cake for 1 month before eating, the flavour improves considerably.

8oz (225g) butter
8oz (225g) light soft brown sugar
2oz (55g) molasses or black treacle
4 eggs
14oz (400g) plain flour
1/2 teaspoon (1/2×5ml) bicarbonate of soda
1 1/2 teaspoons (1 1/2×5ml) grated nutmeg
1 1/2 teaspoons (1 1/2×5ml) ground cloves

1 teaspoon (1×5ml) ground cinnamon
5fl oz (150ml) buttermilk
1 1/2lb (700g) seedless raisins
1 1/4lb (600g) currants
4oz (115g) dates, chopped
4oz (115g) mixed candied peel, chopped
2oz (55g) almonds, blanched and slivered

Cream the butter with the sugar until light and fluffy. Mix in the treacle and the eggs, beating well between each addition. Add the flour sieved with the bicarbonate of soda, nutmeg, cloves and cinnamon and mix in the buttermilk. Stir in the raisins, currants, dates, candied peel and almonds until well combined. Turn the mixture into a lined and greased 8in (20cm) square tin and smooth level. Make slight dip in the centre of the mixture and tie a band of double-layer brown paper around the tin, protruding 3–4in (7.5–10cm) above the rim. This helps to prevent the top from browning too much. Bake the cake in a slow oven (300°F, 150°C; Gas Mark 2) for 2 hours. Reduce the heat to 275°F (140°C; Gas Mark 1) and bake the cake for a further 45–60 minutes or until a thin wooden skewer comes out clean from the centre of the cake. Cool the cake in the tin.

To decorate the cake, either leave it plain, or marzipan and ice in the usual way. Or apply a layer of marzipan only and make a pattern around the edge by pressing in the prongs of a fork, then brush the marzipan with egg yolk and brown it slightly under a hot grill. In the centre arrange marzipan fruits, or nuts and glacé fruits.

DUNDEE · CAKE

Scotland has a fine reputation for baking and this fruit cake from Dundee with its almond-encrusted top is its most famous cake. A Dundee cake, stored in an air-tight container in a cold place, keeps well for 1–2 months.

6oz (170g) butter
6oz (170g) caster sugar or light
  brown sugar
3 eggs
Zest of orange
8oz (225g) plain flour
1 teaspoon (1×5ml) baking powder
1 teaspoon (1×5ml) mixed spice
  (optional)
2oz (55g) ground almonds
6oz (170g) sultanas

4oz (115g) seedless raisins
4oz (115g) currants
3oz (85g) glacé cherries, quartered
2oz (55g) candied orange peel,
  chopped
1–2oz (30–55g) blanched
  almonds, halved
1–2 tablespoons (1–2×15ml) milk
  or whisky
A little egg white to glaze

Cream the butter and sugar until light and fluffy. Beat in the eggs, one at a time, with the zest of orange. Fold in the flour sieved with the baking powder and mixed spice. Mix in the ground almonds, sultanas, raisins, currants, glacé cherries and candied peel. The mixture should be fairly stiff. Add the milk or whisky if you think it necessary. Turn the mixture into a greased and base-lined 7in (18cm) tin and smooth the top level. Arrange the almonds — their pointed ends to the centre — on top. Start with a ring of almonds almost touching at the outside of the cake. Place a second ring inside the first and then a third smaller ring. Usually there is only room for three or four almonds in the very centre of the cake. Bake the cake in a slow oven (325°F, 160°C; Gas Mark 3) for 2 hours. The cake is cooked when a fine wooden skewer comes out of the centre clean. Cool the cake in the tin but while it is still warm brush the top with lightly beaten egg white to give it a shiny finish.

WHITE · FRUIT · CAKE

Some young children don't really care for the traditional dark, rich fruit cake. They do, however, enjoy this fruit cake with its brightly coloured assorted glacé fruits. A white fruit cake is also suitable for Christmas and other celebrations.

8oz (225g) butter
5oz (140g) caster sugar
4 large eggs
4oz (115g) plain flour
4oz (115g) self-raising flour
2oz (55g) cornflour
6oz (170g) glacé cherries, quartered
4oz (115g) glacé pineapple, roughly chopped
4oz (115g) mixed glacé fruits, roughly chopped

2oz (55g) crystallised ginger, chopped
2oz (55g) candied peel, chopped
2oz (55g) angelica, diced
2oz (55g) blanched almonds, sliced
2oz (55g) blanched hazelnuts, roughly chopped
1 tablespoon (1 × 15ml) lemon or pineapple juice

Cream the butter and sugar until light and fluffy. Gradually beat in the eggs, if necessary adding a little of the flour to prevent curdling. Fold in the sieved flours and then mix in all the mixed fruit and nuts with the lemon juice. Turn the mixture into a greased and lined 8in (20cm) cake tin. Smooth the top level, then make a slight hollow in the centre. Tie a double layer of brown paper around the tin wide enough to protrude 3in (7.5cm) above the rim of the tin. Bake the cake in a slow oven (325°F, 160°C; Gas Mark 3) for 2–2½ hours or until a thin wooden skewer comes out clean from the centre of the cake. Cool in the tin for 30 minutes, then turn on to a wire rack.

· Biscuits and Cookies ·

The earliest recorded biscuits were probably the wafers of the four-
teenth century. 'Wafers piping hot out of the gleed,' wrote Geoffrey
Chaucer. These were made out of very fine flour and were baked on
a wafer iron held over the fire. The word biscuit comes from the
French meaning *twice cooked*. And it may be that early hard-baked
biscuits like ship's biscuits were in fact baked twice in order to obtain
the degree of dryness necessary to survive as 'hard tack' for the
duration of a long voyage. Of course, 'hard tack' is, I hope, a long way
from the kind of biscuit that we like to bake at home today. The name
biscuit, or *bisket* as it appeared in eighteenth-century cookery books,
was given to a wide range of flat, cooked mixtures. The term was even
given to fruit purées, often of quince or orange, which were dried in
a flat sheet and then cut into smaller shapes. And up until Tudor
times biscuits were still often referred to as cakes.

One of the earliest recipes for Shrewsbury cakes appeared in 1561
but it is thought that the biscuits date from far earlier. Brandy snaps
are even older; these are our present-day equivalent of the medieval
gauffres and were made on a flat metal sheet over the open fire. As
soon as they were cooked to a golden brown they were lifted from the
baking sheet and wrapped around a wooden stick to set into the
curled shape that we still appreciate. Crisp, buttery Scottish
shortbread which was originally made with oatmeal dates from the
twelfth century and possibly earlier. This biscuit was usually made in
a circular shape to represent the sun and the pinched edge that we still
make on shortbread was supposed to represent the sun's rays. At some
time a smaller circle was cut from the centre of a round of shortbread
and the remaining ring was cut into eight wedges which were called
petty cotes tallis; these we now call 'petticoat tails'. Indeed, each wedge
does resemble a full petticoat or skirt. Later still, shortbread was
pressed into wooden moulds to leave a raised pattern, most commonly of the national emblem — a Scottish thistle — on the surface
of the biscuit.

Spiced biscuits were very popular. Ginger was the spice most
widely used and these biscuits were made in a variety of shapes. A
tradition grew for selling ginger biscuits at hiring and mop fairs and
on feast days. In Devon, at the great annual fairs like the Tavistock

Goose Fair or Bampton Pony Fair or on Honiton Hot Penny Day, gingerbread men and ginger biscuits known as *fairings* were sold from a small booth or a biscuit carrier who peddled his ware from a basket.

Cookies have come to us from America. Defining the difference between a cookie and a biscuit is almost impossible. On some occasions a cookie is softer and more cake-like than a biscuit and on others a cookie is hardly distinguishable from a biscuit. On the whole the term depends on where the cookie or biscuit originates. What perhaps matters more is that they taste equally delicious.

HONEY · LACE · BISCUITS · *(makes about 30)*

These crisp biscuits which resemble brandy-snaps are cooled over a rolling pin to give them their curved shape.

4oz (115g) honey
4oz (115g) butter
3oz (85g) plain flour
1/4 teaspoon (1/4×5ml) salt

2oz (55g) caster sugar
1/2 teaspoon (1/2×5ml) vanilla
* essence*

Measure the honey into a pan and heat until almost boiling. Remove from the heat and add the butter cut in pieces. Stir until melted. Mix in the flour sieved with the salt, the sugar and the vanilla essence to make a smooth batter. Drop well-spaced teaspoons of the mixture on to a greased baking sheet. Bake in a moderate oven (375°F, 190°C; Gas Mark 5) for 6–8 minutes until golden brown. Cool on the baking sheet for 1 minute, then lift off with a spatula and place over a rolling pin. Leave until cool and set into shape. Transfer to a wire rack. If the biscuits harden before you have time to shape them replace them in the oven for a few minutes to soften.

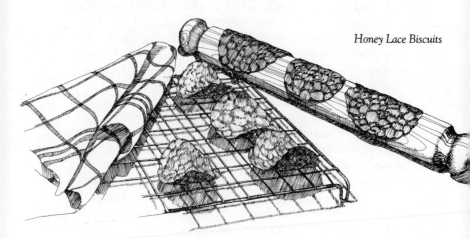

Honey Lace Biscuits

MARYSES · *(makes about 30)*

Piped biscuits always look well finished. These little morsels melt in the mouth. They are very good plain or sandwiched with buttercream and go well with ice-cream or a sorbet.

4oz (115g) butter	*Pinch of baking powder*
1oz (30g) icing sugar	*1 or 2 drops vanilla essence*
4oz (115g) plain flour	*(optional)*

Soften the butter in a mixing bowl and beat until creamy. Mix in the sieved icing sugar and the flour sieved with the baking powder. Flavour with the vanilla essence if you wish. Spoon the mixture into a forcing bag fitted with a star nozzle. Pipe small rosettes on to a buttered and floured baking sheet. Bake in the centre of a moderate oven (375°F, 190°C; Gas Mark 5) for 9–12 minutes until the biscuits are pale gold at the edges. Cool on a wire rack.

GINGER · FAIRINGS · *(makes 30)*

4oz (115g) butter	*1 teaspoon (1×5ml) ground ginger*
1oz (30g) golden syrup	*1/2 teaspoon (1/2×5ml)*
3oz (85g) light soft brown sugar	*bicarbonate of soda*
6oz (170g) plain flour	

Measure the butter and syrup into a pan and melt over a low heat. Remove from the heat and stir in the sugar. Add the flour sieved with the ginger and bicarbonate of soda and mix until well combined. Take teaspoons of the mixture and roll into balls, then flatten on to an ungreased non-stick baking sheet. Bake in a moderate oven (375°F, 190°C; Gas Mark 5) for 10–12 minutes. Cool on the baking sheet for 2–3 minutes, then transfer to a wire rack.

PARLIAMENT · CAKES · OR · PARLIES · *(makes 20)*

Parlies are highly delicious ginger biscuits which were once sold from stalls in the streets of Edinburgh. They are said to have taken their name from the members of the Scottish parliament.

4oz (115g) butter	*8oz (225g) plain flour*
4oz (115g) brown sugar	*1–2 teaspoons (1–2×5ml) ground*
4oz (115g) black treacle	*ginger*

Cream the butter with the sugar and treacle until light. Gradually work in the flour sieved with the ground ginger to make a stiff dough. Drop teaspoons of the mixture on to a greased baking sheet and bake in a moderate oven (325°F, 170°C; Gas Mark 3) for 15–20 minutes. Transfer to a wire rack to cool.

GINGERBREAD · PEOPLE · *(makes 12)*

Gingerbread men and women are part of most people's childhood. In *Lark Rise to Candleford* Flora Thompson remembers them on sale at a stall in her Oxfordshire village towards the end of the nineteenth century. And the cookery writer, Ambrose Heath, wrote thirty years ago, 'It may seem rather old-fashioned to suggest a revival of those jolly little gingerbread boys that I remember so well in my childhood, with their primitive attraction (like that of the Cerne Abbas giant) and their currants for eyes and buttons.' Recently gingerbread people have become very popular again.

8oz (225g) self-raising flour
3oz (85g) dark muscovado sugar
2 teaspoons (2×5ml) ground
   ginger
1 teaspoon (1×5ml) mixed spice

½ teaspoon (½×5ml) salt
4oz (115g) butter
3–4 tablespoons (3–4×15ml) milk
Currants for eyes and buttons
White icing (optional)

Sieve the flour, sugar, ginger, mixed spice and salt into a mixing bowl. Rub in the butter until it resembles breadcrumbs. Mix to a dough with the milk. Roll out the dough on a floured board until ¼in (6mm) thick. Use a gingerbread man and woman cutter to cut out as many biscuits as possible. Place on a greased baking sheet and press the currants into the biscuits for eyes and buttons. Bake in a moderately hot oven (400°F, 200°C; Gas Mark 6) for 15 minutes. Cool on a baking sheet for 2 minutes, then carefully transfer to a wire tray to cool completely. Decorate the biscuits with piped icing, if you wish.

Gingerbread People

BETSY · PINNEY'S · ANIMAL · BISCUITS · *(makes about 30)*
When I was first asked to write this book I mentioned it to some friends in the village. A few days later they kindly handed me a sheaf of hand-written pages in which Betsy Pinney recalls her years of cooking for children. She writes, 'This is the basic recipe for the biscuits I make. There are, of course, innumerable other varieties, but I chose this because someone gave me the recipe and my children wanted to do something *real*, one cold, wet, winter afternoon. So I put the ingredients in two basins and let them mix it up with their hands (duly washed). The result was an unqualified success — I've used it ever since. The biscuits are very easy to make but are rather sweet for adult taste.' I serve the biscuits plain or outlined with piped icing.

4oz (115g) butter	*4oz (115g) icing sugar*
4oz (115g) caster sugar	*Hot water*
2 egg yolks	*Food colouring*
5oz (140g) plain flour	

Cream the butter and sugar, add the egg yolks and mix well. Mix in the sieved flour with a wooden spoon until the mixture forms a soft dough. Gather into a ball. On a well-floured board roll out half the dough at a time to ¼in (5mm) thickness and cut out the animal shapes using special cutters. Place well apart on a greased baking sheet. Bake in a slow oven (300°F, 150°C; Gas Mark 2) for 15–20 minutes until pale brown. Cool on the baking sheet for 2 minutes, then transfer to a wire rack.

Sieve the icing sugar into a bowl and mix in hot water to make a thin piping icing. Colour it if you wish. Pipe a fine line around the edge of each biscuit. Then add an eye or any additional and appropriate features like a wing, ear or tail. Store these biscuits in an airtight container to keep them crisp.

Alphabet and Numeral Biscuits are easily made from the same mixture.

BACHELOR'S · BUTTONS · *(makes at least 50)*
These miniature biscuits are suitable for a doll's tea party. The biscuit dough also works well for piped or pressed biscuits.

2oz (55g) butter	*4oz (115g) plain flour*
3oz (85g) caster sugar	*1 egg yolk*
Few drops of vanilla essence or a	*Vanilla butter icing (optional)*
little grated zest of orange or lemon	

Cream the butter with the sugar until light and fluffy. Beat in the vanilla essence and gradually work in the sieved flour with the yolk of egg to make a soft dough. Take a coffee-spoon of the mixture and roll into a ball. Place on a greased and floured baking sheet and bake in a moderate oven (350°F, 180°C; Gas Mark 4) for 8–10 minutes until pale brown. Cool on the baking sheet.

The biscuits can be served plain or they can be sandwiched with vanilla butter icing.

CINNAMON · STARS · *(makes about 24)*

Star-shaped biscuits are usually reserved for Christmas. In the Shetland Isles, star biscuits are made with circles cut in the centre. If you wish to tie these biscuits on the Christmas tree remember to make a hole in them for a ribbon.

3 egg whites
6oz (170g) icing sugar
8oz (225g) ground almonds
1 teaspoon (1 × 5ml) grated zest of lemon

2–3 teaspoons (2–3 × 5ml) ground cinnamon
A little extra caster sugar

Whisk the egg whites with the sieved icing sugar in a mixing bowl set over simmering water until the mixture is thick and foamy. Remove from the heat and set aside 3 tablespoons (3 × 15ml) of the meringue until later. Fold the ground almonds, zest of lemon and cinnamon into the meringue and stand the bowl in cold water for about 30 minutes until the mixture is cool. Then carefully roll out the mixture on a surface lightly dusted with caster sugar until ¼in (5mm) thick. Use a star cutter to cut out the biscuits. Place on a greased baking sheet and spread or brush the reserved meringue over each biscuit. Bake in a slow oven (325°F, 160°C; Gas Mark 3) for 15–20 minutes until just set. Cool on the baking sheet and then transfer to a wire rack.

PADDINGTON · BEAR · BISCUITS · *(makes 8–10)*

If you can, use a Paddington Bear cutter to make these biscuits, otherwise make a template by tracing a picture of this famous bear. The chocolate icing incorporates Paddington's favourite food — marmalade.

3oz (85g) butter
5oz (140g) caster sugar
1 small egg, beaten
2 tablespoons (2 × 15ml) cocoa
2 tablespoons (2 × 15ml) hot water
6oz (170g) plain flour

Icing:
5oz (140g) plain dessert chocolate
2 tablespoons (2 × 15ml) orange jelly marmalade
2oz (55g) icing sugar
A little hot water

Cream the butter with the sugar until light and fluffy. Beat in the egg and the cocoa blended with the hot water. Add the sieved flour and mix together until the dough forms a ball. Roll out on a floured surface until ¼in (6mm) thick and cut out the biscuits. Bake on a greased baking sheet in a moderately hot oven (400°F, 200°C; Gas Mark 6) for 10–12 minutes until just starting to change colour at the edges. Cool the biscuits on the baking sheet, then transfer to a wire rack.

For the icing, break the chocolate into pieces and melt with the marmalade over hot water. Stir until smooth, then spoon the icing over the hat and boots of each biscuit bear (sometimes I cover the paws too). Mix the icing sugar with sufficient hot water to make a thin piping icing. Spoon this into a forcing bag fitted with a fine line nozzle. Pipe a line to outline the clothes and the face of each biscuit bear.

ELEVENTH · HOUR · KISSES · *(makes 24)*

These macaroon-like biscuits with the charming name can be served plain or sandwiched with whipped cream or butter icing.

2 egg whites	*4oz (115g) finely chopped dried*
4oz (115g) caster sugar	*apricots or dates*
3oz (85g) ground almonds	*A little extra caster sugar for*
	sprinkling

Whisk the egg whites until stiff. Whisk in half the sugar, then fold in the remaining sugar. Mix in the ground almonds with the apricots or dates. Drop dessertspoons of the mixture on to a greased baking tray and sprinkle with caster sugar. Bake in a slow oven (300°F, 150°C; Gas Mark 2) for about 30 minutes until pale gold. Cool on the tray for 5 minutes, then transfer to a wire rack to cool.

HAZELNUT · MACAROONS · *(makes 18)*

These delicately nutty morsels are sandwiched with coffee butter-cream.

4oz (115g) hazelnuts, preferably	*Buttercream:*
still in their thin brown skins	*2oz (55g) butter*
1oz (30g) almonds, blanched	*2oz (55g) caster sugar*
2 egg whites	*1 teaspoon (1 × 5ml) instant coffee,*
6oz (170g) caster sugar	*liquid or powder*
1oz (30g) plain flour	*1 tablespoon (1 × 15ml) hot water*
	Vanilla essence
	1 teaspoon (1 × 5ml) icing sugar

Spread the hazelnuts on a baking sheet and bake in a low oven for 4–5 minutes until the thin brown skins are crisp and the nuts are just changing colour. Cool slightly, then tip the nuts into a cloth and rub off the skins. Chop the hazelnuts and the almonds finely, ideally in a food processor or blender. Whisk the egg whites until stiff then whisk in half the sugar. Mix the chopped nuts with the remaining sugar and the flour and gently fold into the egg whites. Place dessertspoons of the mixture on a baking sheet lined with vegetable parchment making sure they are well spaced. Bake in a slow oven (325°F, 160°C; Gas Mark 3) for 25–30 minutes until firm but just changing colour at the edges. Cool for 2–3 minutes, then carefully transfer to a wire rack to cool.

To make the buttercream; cream the butter with the sugar until pale and creamy. Mix the coffee with the hot water and gradually beat into the butter until the sugar dissolves and the buttercream is smooth. Flavour with a drop of vanilla essence. Sandwich the macaroons with the buttercream and dust lightly with icing sugar.

COCONUT · RINGS · *(makes 30 single biscuits)*

4oz (115g) plain flour	*4oz (115g) desiccated coconut,*
4oz (115g) soft light brown sugar	*unsweetened*
4oz (115g) butter	*1 small egg, beaten*

Sieve the flour and sugar into a bowl and rub in the butter until the mixture resembles breadcrumbs. Stir in the coconut and mix to a dough with the egg. Lightly knead the dough into a ball. Roll out the dough thinly on a floured surface. Cut into rounds with a 2½in (6.5cm) fluted biscuit cutter. Use a 1in (2.5cm) cutter to remove the centre of each biscuit. Place the rings on a greased baking sheet and bake in a moderate oven (375°F, 190°C; Gas Mark 5) for 8–12 minutes. Cool the biscuits on a wire rack.

Variation:
Chocolate Coconut Rings Break 3½oz (100g) of plain dessert chocolate into pieces and melt in a bowl set over hot water. Dip half of each biscuit in the chocolate and leave on a wire rack until set. Alternatively, sandwich the biscuits with the melted chocolate.

CHOCOLATE · JUMBLES · *(makes about 36)*
Jumbles are reputed to date from the fifteenth century — it is said that the recipe was dropped on the battlefield at Bosworth. This is my chocolate version for today which moulds easily into the traditional S shape or into any other letter or initial.

6½oz (190g) plain flour
1½oz (45g) cocoa
¼ teaspoon (¼×5ml) ground
    cinnamon
4oz (115g) caster sugar
5oz (140g) butter

1 large egg, beaten
2oz (55g) granulated sugar
3½oz (100g) plain dessert
    chocolate
2–3 tablespoons (2–3×15ml) milk

Sieve the flour, cocoa and ground cinnamon into a bowl. Mix in the caster sugar and rub in the butter until the mixture resembles breadcrumbs. Add the beaten egg and mix to a dough. Take a heaped teaspoon of the mixture and roll in your hand to form a sausage. Dip in the granulated sugar and place on a greased baking sheet in the form of a letter S, or in a variety of letters or numerals if you prefer. Bake in a moderate oven (350°F, 180°C; Gas Mark 4) for 12–15 minutes. Remove from the baking sheet with a flexible knife and cool on a wire rack.

Break the chocolate into pieces and melt in a bowl over simmering water. Mix in the milk to thin the chocolate slightly. Dribble melted chocolate over the biscuits or dip each end into the chocolate. Place on a wire rack and leave until set.

LEMON · CREAM · COOKIES · (makes 18)

4oz (115g) butter
3oz (85g) icing sugar
1–2 drops vanilla essence
5oz (140g) self-raising flour
2½oz (70g) cornflour
2 tablespoons (2×15ml) milk

Filling:
3oz (85g) cream cheese
1oz (30g) caster sugar
Finely grated zest of ½ lemon
1 egg yolk
1½oz (45g) currants
½oz (15g) candied lemon peel,
    finely chopped
A little extra icing sugar

Cream the butter with the icing sugar until light and fluffy. Beat in the vanilla essence and gradually mix in the flour sieved with the cornflour. Mix to a soft dough with half the milk and knead into a ball. Wrap in cling film and chill while you prepare the filling.

Mix the cream cheese with the caster sugar, the zest of lemon and half the egg yolk. Stir in the currants and lemon peel. Roll out the dough until ⅛in (3mm) thick and cut out circles with a 2½in (6.5cm) fluted cookie cutter. Place half the circles on a greased baking sheet and place a teaspoon of filling in the centre of each. Brush the edges with the rest of the egg yolk mixed with the remaining milk and cover with the other circles. Press the edges together and brush the cookies with the egg mixture. Bake in the centre of a moderate oven (350°F, 180°C; Gas Mark 4) for 20–25 minutes until golden brown at the edges. Cool on the baking sheet for a few minutes, then transfer to a wire rack. Dust the cookies with icing sugar shaken through a fine sieve.

NUT · BROWNIES · (makes 16)

These small fudgy squares are a classic children's cake. This definite winner comes from a friend, Anne Collieu.

6oz (170g) butter	2 eggs
2 tablespoons (2 × 15ml) cocoa	2oz (55g) plain flour
6oz (170g) caster sugar	2oz (55g) walnuts, chopped

Melt 2oz (55g) of the butter with the cocoa and mix until smooth, then set aside to cool. Cream the remaining butter with the sugar until light and fluffy. Beat in the eggs and the cocoa mixture. Fold in the flour and walnuts. Turn the mixture into a 7in (18cm) square greased baking tin. Bake in a moderate oven (350°F, 180°C; Gas Mark 4) for 35–45 minutes. Cool in the tin and cut into squares.

SCOTT · EWING'S · FAVOURITE · BROWNIES ·
(makes 24 squares)

On the basis that you can't have too much of a good thing, I am also including a brownie recipe from an American friend. These brownies also taste terrific — they are lighter in texture, not so fudgy and are more cake-like.

4oz (115g) unsalted butter	4oz (115g) plain flour
8oz (225g) caster sugar	Large pinch of salt
2 eggs, separated	4fl oz (100ml) milk
2oz (55g) unsweetened or bitter chocolate (eg Baker's), melted	4oz (115g) pecans or walnuts, chopped (optional)
1 teaspoon (1 × 5ml) vanilla essence	3–4oz (85–115g) plain dessert chocolate, grated

Cream the butter with the sugar and beat in the egg yolks, the melted chocolate and the vanilla essence. Fold in the flour sieved with the salt alternately with the milk. Whisk the egg whites until stiff and fold into the mixture with the chopped pecans or walnuts. Turn the mixture into a buttered and floured 8in (20cm) square tin. Bake in a moderate oven (350°F, 180°C; Gas Mark 4) for 30 minutes. Remove from the oven and immediately sprinkle the grated chocolate over the top. As soon as it melts spread evenly. Cool the brownies in the tin, then cut into squares.

CELIA'S · MOOSE · HALL · CARAMEL · FINGERS ·
(makes 24)

These caramel biscuits are a speciality of the Women's Institute home-baking stall in the Moose Hall in Tiverton, Devon.

4oz (115g) butter
2oz (55g) caster sugar
6oz (170g) self-raising flour

Topping:
7oz (200g) condensed milk
4oz (115g) butter

2oz (55g) caster sugar
2 tablespoons (2 × 15ml) golden syrup
1/4 teaspoon (1/4 × 5ml) vanilla essence
7oz (200g) plain dessert chocolate, melted

Cream the butter with the caster sugar until light and fluffy. Gradually work in the sieved flour to make a soft dough. Press the dough into a greased 10×7in (25×18cm) non-stick baking tin and smooth level with the back of a wooden spoon. Bake in a moderate oven (350°F, 180°C; Gas Mark 4) for 10–15 minutes until golden brown. Cool in the tin.

Gently heat the condensed milk with the butter, caster sugar and golden syrup until the sugar has dissolved. Bring to the boil and cook, stirring, for 5 minutes. Remove from the heat and mix in the vanilla essence. Cool the mixture until the caramel starts to thicken then pour over the biscuit base in an even layer. Cover with the melted chocolate. As it cools make a pattern in the chocolate with the blade of a knife. When set cut into fingers.

CHOCOLATE · DIGESTIVE · BISCUITS · *(makes 18)*

Nearly everyone likes chocolate digestives, and these biscuits are just as delicious served plain without chocolate.

6oz (170g) wholemeal flour
2oz (55g) muscovado sugar

4oz (115g) butter
5oz (140g) plain dessert chocolate

Measure the flour into a mixing bowl and stir in the sugar making sure there are no lumps. Rub in the butter until the mixture resembles breadcrumbs, then knead the mixture into a ball. Roll out thinly until 1/8in (3mm) thick and use a 2 1/2in (6.5cm) cutter to cut out the biscuits. Bake on a greased baking sheet in a moderate oven for 12–15 minutes or until the edges are changing colour. Cool on the baking sheet for 3–4 minutes, then transfer to a wire rack to cool.

Break the chocolate into pieces and melt in a bowl over hot water. Spoon chocolate over the biscuits and place on a wire rack until set.

POINSETTIA · PETAL · COOKIES · *(makes 18)*

4oz (115g) butter
2oz (55g) light soft brown sugar
1 egg, separated
1 tablespoon (1×15ml) lemon
    juice

6oz (170g) plain flour
2 teaspoons (2×5ml) caster sugar
3oz (85g) finely chopped walnuts
3 large glacé cherries, each cut
    into 8 segments

Cream the butter with the sugar until light and fluffy. Beat in the egg yolk and the lemon juice. Mix in the sieved flour to make a soft dough. In another bowl whisk the egg white until stiff, then whisk in the sugar. Take a rounded teaspoon of the mixture and form into a ball. Dip in the egg white, then roll in the chopped walnuts until completely coated. Place on a greased baking sheet and arrange three pieces of glacé cherry on top to resemble a poinsettia. Bake in a moderate oven (350°F, 180°C; Gas Mark 4) for about 20 minutes until crisp and golden. Transfer to a wire rack to cool.

FLORENTINES · *(makes 18)*

Did Catherine de Medici introduce us to this lovely little biscuit? She arrived in France in the sixteenth century to become the bride of Henry II and brought with her a full retinue of Italian chefs. She is credited with introducing many new recipes and dishes. If she brought these biscuits they would have been plain and without their coating of chocolate. These biscuits make a particularly delightful present, arranged in a small box and tied with pretty ribbon.

1½oz (45g) unsalted butter
2oz (55g) caster sugar
½oz (15g) plain flour
1 tablespoon (1×15ml) double
    cream
1 teaspoon (1×5ml) lemon juice
2oz (55g) candied orange peel,
    chopped

1½oz (45g) glacé cherries, sliced
1oz (30g) sultanas
½oz (15g) candied angelica, diced
2oz (55g) blanched almonds,
    slivered
6oz (170g) plain dessert chocolate

Melt the butter with the sugar in a pan over medium heat. Remove from the heat and beat in the sieved flour, cream and lemon juice. Stir in the candied orange peel, cherries, sultanas, angelica and almonds. Place rounded teaspoons of the mixture on a baking sheet lined with nonstick baking paper, allowing room for the biscuits to spread. Bake in a moderate oven (350°F, 180°C; Gas Mark 4) for 10–15 minutes until golden brown, taking care not to overcook. Cool the biscuits on the baking sheet, then carefully peel off the paper and place on a wire rack.

Melt the chocolate in a bowl over hot water. Spread a thin layer of chocolate on the underside of each biscuit. When half-set drag the prongs of a fork across the chocolate in a zig-zag pattern to give a combed effect. Leave the biscuits on a wire rack until set. To keep florentines crisp, store them in an air-tight plastic box or bag.

CHINESE · CHEWS · *(makes 24)*

This is a recipe from my own childhood and comes from one of my mother's Canadian cookbooks.

3oz (85g) plain flour
1 teaspoon (1×5ml) baking powder
Good pinch of salt
4oz (115g) demerara sugar
5oz (140g) dates, chopped

3½oz (100g) walnuts, chopped
2 eggs, beaten
A little extra demerara sugar for
  sprinkling

Sieve the flour, baking powder and salt into a bowl. Add the sugar, dates and walnuts and mix in the beaten eggs until the ingredients are well combined. Spread the mixture evenly in a greased non-stick Swiss-roll tin 11×7in (28×18cm) and sprinkle with the extra demerara sugar. Bake in a moderate oven (350°F, 180°C; Gas Mark 4) for 25–30 minutes. Remove from the oven and mark into 24 squares. Cool in the tin and cut through when cold.

SHREWSBURY · CAKES · *(makes 20)*

The first reference we have for Shrewsbury cakes dates from 1561. At that time biscuits were known as cakes. This recipe, which contains two favourite Elizabethan flavours, rosewater and nutmeg, is slightly adapted from John Murrell's version which was published in 1621.

8oz (85g) plain flour
4oz (115g) caster sugar
½ teaspoon (½×5ml) finely
  grated nutmeg

6oz (170g) butter
1–2 tablespoons (1–2×15ml)
  rosewater

Sieve the flour into a bowl and stir in the sugar and nutmeg. Add the butter cut in pieces. Rub in, as when making pastry, until the mixture resembles breadcrumbs. Add sufficient rosewater, mixing it in with a knife until the mixture forms a ball of dough. Roll out the dough on a floured surface to ⅛in (3mm) thickness and cut out the biscuits with a 3in (7.5cm) plain round cutter. Place on a floured baking sheet and cover the biscuits with a sheet of greaseproof paper. Bake in a slow oven (325°F, 160°C; Gas Mark 3) for 15–20 minutes or until firm. The biscuits should hardly change colour. Cool on the baking sheet, then transfer to a wire rack.

PITCATHLEY · SHORTBREAD · *(makes 16–20 pieces)*

This unusual Scottish shortbread contains currants and candied peel which gives it a lemon flavour and an unusual texture. The recipe comes from a charming little book published fifty years ago called *Five O'Clock Cakes and Pastries*.

6oz (170g) butter
3oz (85g) caster sugar
8oz (225g) plain flour
2oz (55g) currants
1oz (30g) candied lemon peel,
    finely diced

1oz (30g) candied orange peel,
    finely diced
A little extra caster sugar

Cream the butter until soft, then beat in the sugar until the mixture is fairly light and fluffy. Add the flour, currants and candied peel and mix together with a wooden spoon until the mixture forms a ball. Knead lightly with your fingers then divide the dough in two. Roll out each piece to make a 7in (18cm) circle. Transfer to a greased baking sheet allowing room for the shortbread to spread during baking. Prick all over with a fork and mark into 8 or 10 wedges. Make a crimped pattern around the outside with your fingertips. Bake in a slow oven (325°F, 160°C; Gas Mark 3) for about 25 minutes until pale gold. Cool on the baking sheet for a few minutes, then cut into portions and transfer to a wire rack to cool. Dust with caster sugar.

Pitcathley Shortbread

· Sweetmeats ·

On that little old stall with its canvas awning . . . stood a box filled with thin dark brown slabs packed in pink paper. 'What is that brown sweet?' asked Laura, spelling out the word 'Chocolate'. A visiting cousin, being fairly well educated and a great reader, already knew it by name. 'Oh, that's chocolate,' he said off-handedly. 'But don't buy any; it's for drinking. They have it for breakfast in France.' A year or so later, chocolate was a favourite sweet even in a place as remote as the hamlet . . .

It is not often that the arrival of a new delicacy is as deftly noted as Flora Thompson relates in *Lark Rise in Candleford*. The time was the late nineteenth century and the place her small Oxfordshire hamlet of Lark Rise. Now that chocolate figures so strongly in most manufactured sweets I suspect that most of us, a hundred years or so further on, are surprised to learn that a bar of chocolate arrived so late in rural Oxfordshire. The first chocolate house had opened in London in 1657 but a high customs duty kept chocolate as a drink for the rich until 1828. And it was another fifty years before a Swiss, M. Peter, produced a successful milk chocolate by mixing condensed milk with dark bitter chocolate.

Man had discovered his fondness for sweet, sticky food thousands of years earlier. Honey and dried fruits, especially dates which when compressed yield a brown honey-like syrup, provided the sweetener in man's earliest diet. Sweetmeats or sweets, as they are now more commonly called, came originally from the Near East, mainly from the Arab world, during the twelfth and thirteenth centuries. The crusaders brought back exotic spices and perfumes, scented flower waters and sweetmeats. Some of these sweetmeats such as Turkish Delight and the jellied Quince Paste have never lost their charm. We still make and enjoy eating them today. We frequently make them as gifts for family and friends. I imagine there can be few grandparents, aunts or uncles who have not, at some time, received a small box or dish of chocolate truffles, stuffed dates, squares of fudge or coconut ice, perhaps a little mis-shapen, but made with extreme care and concentration by children who wanted to show their love and affection on the occasion of a birthday or at Christmas.

Making sweets at home has always been a frivolous and pleasurable side of cookery. In the sixteenth century sweetmaking was regarded as a branch of preserving. Apricots and plums in particular were cooked until they formed a thick purée which was dried in the sun or near the fire until firm enough to be cut into small pieces. These little *fruit cakes* or *tablet* were stored in air-tight jars or boxes and were served as a treat at the end of a meal, especially at festivals and feasts. They also appeared on the table at the Tudor *banquet*, the name given to the separate course of sweet foods and delicacies eaten some time after the main meal and often served in a specially built room or building. In the eighteenth century homemade sweetmeats were sometimes taken on journeys. Lady Castlehill in 1712 says of her sweetmeats made from a dried purée of oranges which she called *orange bisket*, 'You may carry them in your Pocket without offence.'

VANILLA · FUDGE

Fudge has long been associated with the Westcountry where the rich cream and milk give this soft sweetmeat a fine flavour. This recipe uses condensed milk which should give a reliable result.

14oz (400g) condensed milk
1lb (450g) granulated sugar
4oz (115g) unsalted butter

2oz (55g) golden syrup
1/2 teaspoon (1/2 × 5ml) vanilla
essence

Measure the milk, sugar, butter and syrup into a heavy-based pan and place over a moderate heat. Stir until the sugar has dissolved. Raise the heat and boil, stirring all the time, until the syrup reaches 237°F (114°C) or the *soft ball* stage. Remove from the heat, mix in the vanilla essence and pour the fudge into a buttered non-stick baking tin. When half-set mark into squares and cut through when cold.

CUMBERLAND · COFFEE · NUT · FUDGE

1lb (450g) soft light brown sugar
8oz (225g) butter
7oz (200g) condensed milk
1 tablespoon (1 × 15ml) liquid
coffee essence

2oz (55g) roasted hazelnuts,
roughly chopped

Measure the sugar and butter into a heavy-based pan and stir over a low heat until the sugar is dissolved. Add the condensed milk and slowly bring to the boil, stirring well. Boil steadily for 15 minutes, stirring all the time. Remove from the heat and mix in the coffee essence and the nuts. Pour the fudge into a buttered dish or tin. Leave until cold, then cut the fudge into squares.

EDINBURGH · BUTTERSCOTCH

Towards the end of the seventeenth century raw sugar began to be imported in bulk from the West Indies. Scotland then started its sugar-refining industry and thus the Scots developed their famous sweet tooth.

1lb (450g) brown sugar	*½ teaspoon (½ × 5ml) ground*
4 tablespoons (4 × 15ml) cold water	*ginger*
4oz (115g) unsalted butter	*1 teaspoon (1 × 5ml) cold water*

Measure the brown sugar and the water into a heavy-based pan and stir over a low heat until dissolved. Add the butter in pieces and bring the mixture to the boil. Cook until 247°F (119°C) or *firm ball* stage. Mix the ginger with the water and add to the syrup and mix in with a fork. Pour the butterscotch into a buttered non-stick 6in (15cm) square cake tin and when slightly cooled, mark into squares. Leave until cold, then tap gently with the back of a spoon and the butterscotch should break into squares.

TURKISH · DELIGHT

Many oriental spices and flavours were brought back to Britain by the crusaders. Elizabethan recipes abound in rose petals and the distilled essence made from them. We have still not lost our enthusiasm for the rosewater which characterises this scented jelly sweetmeat.

1oz (30g) powdered gelatine	*Rosewater*
½pt (300ml) cold water	*A little mild salad oil*
1lb (450g) sugar	*Icing sugar*
Pink food colouring	

Sprinkle the gelatine on to half of the water and dissolve over a low heat. In a heavy-based pan dissolve the sugar in the remaining water, stirring until dissolved but do not allow to boil. Add the gelatine liquid to the syrup and simmer the mixture without stirring for 30 minutes. The mixture is ready when a short thread held between the finger and thumb breaks quickly. Remove from the heat and add a few drops of pink food colouring and rosewater to taste. Pour the mixture into an oiled 6in (15cm) non-stick cake tin and leave in a cool place to set. Turn the jelly on to a board dusted with icing sugar. Cut into squares and place in a box. Dust generously with icing sugar.

Variation:
Peppermint Turkish Delight
Stir a few drops of green colouring and a drop of oil of peppermint into the unflavoured mixture.

TOFFEE · APPLES

No Guy Fawkes bonfire would be complete without toffee apples.
November the Fifth toffee is also known as Plot Toffee, and apples
make an appearance at every winter festival in Britain.

1lb (450g) sugar	*8 small eating apples*
8 tablespoons (8×15ml) cold water	*8 short wooden skewers*

Dissolve the sugar in the water in a heavy-based pan over a low heat.
Stir until the sugar is completely dissolved. Raise the heat and boil
the syrup until it is golden brown and reaches 280°F (137°C) or the
small crack stage. Wipe the apples with a dry cloth to remove any wax
or bloom. Insert a wooden skewer into the stalk end of each apple for
the handle. Dip the apples, one at a time, into the toffee, twisting
until evenly coated, if necessary tilt the pan. Place handle-side up on
waxed paper or vegetable parchment and leave until the toffee is set.
Eat within a few hours, otherwise wrap the toffee apples in cellophane
to prevent the toffee from softening.

HONEYCOMB · TOFFEE

This golden orange toffee full of small holes is always popular.

6oz (170g) granulated sugar	*1 teaspoon (1×5ml) bicarbonate*
2oz (55g) golden syrup	*of soda*
1oz (30g) butter	

Measure the sugar, syrup and butter into a large, heavy-based pan.
Cook, stirring, over a low heat until the sugar is dissolved. Raise the
heat and bring the syrup to 280°F (137°C) or *soft crack* stage. Remove
the pan from the heat and stir in the bicarbonate of soda. The toffee
will froth up immediately. Pour into an oiled non-stick baking tin and
leave to set. Use a small hammer or a wooden mallet to break the
toffee into bite-sized pieces and pack into small plastic bags or an air-
tight plastic box.

HARDBAKE

Charles Dickens tells us that in Victorian times hardbake or almond
brittle was sold in the streets of Rochester and Chatham. ' "The prin-
cipal productions of these towns," says Mr Pickwick, "appear to be
soldiers, sailors, Jews, chalk, shrimps, officers, and dockyard men.
The commodities chiefly exposed for sale in the public streets are
marine stores, hardbake, apples, flat-fish and oysters . . ." '

6oz (170g) blanched almonds,	*½pt (300ml) cold water*
halved	*A pinch of cream of tartar*
1lb (450g) loaf sugar	

Spread the almonds in a single layer on a baking sheet and toast under a hot grill until golden brown. Remove from the heat and set aside. Dissolve the sugar in the water in a heavy-based pan over low heat. Add the cream of tartar and bring the syrup to the boil. Cook until the syrup is orange brown but do not let it turn too dark or the hardbake will be bitter. Remove from the heat and stir in the almonds. Immediately pour into a buttered non-stick baking tin and leave to set. Use a small hammer or a wooden mallet to break the hardbake into bite-sized pieces.

FRESH · COCONUT · ICE

Children are always attracted by the brown furry case of a fresh coconut. This recipe for coconut ice comes from the nineteenth century when the coconut shy was a popular attraction at the travelling fair. To crack open a coconut, first puncture the nut by driving a sharp point through one or two of the 'eyes' at the wider end of the nut. Pour the coconut milk into a measuring jug. Place the coconut on a baking sheet and bake in a moderate oven for 20–30 minutes or until the shell cracks. Remove from the oven and place the nut on a crumpled cloth on a strong surface. Use a hammer to give the coconut a resounding blow which should crack the case into two or three pieces. Use a spoon or fork to prise the moist white flesh out of the brown shell. Remove the brown skin with a vegetable peeler or a knife and grate the white flesh of the nut into a bowl ready for use.

1 medium-sized fresh coconut   *1 tablespoon (1 × 15ml) double cream*
2lb (900g) sugar   *Pink food colouring*

Add sufficient cold water to the coconut milk to measure ½pt (300ml). Pour into a heavy-based pan and add the sugar. Stir over low heat until the sugar has dissolved. Raise the heat and boil the syrup steadily for 10 minutes. Add the grated coconut flesh and cook for a further 10 minutes stirring from time to time. Remove from the heat, mix in the cream and stand the pan in cold water, beating the mixture all the time until it thickens. Pour half into a buttered non-stick oblong cake tin or dish. Add a drop or two of pink food colouring to the remaining mixture to tint it pale pink. Spoon the pink coconut ice over the white layer and spread level. Set aside to cool, then cut into squares.

MARZIPAN

Marzipan is an ancient mixture of ground almonds, fine sugar and the white of egg. The name comes from the medieval word, *marchpane*, which itself derives from the Old French *massepains*. One theory

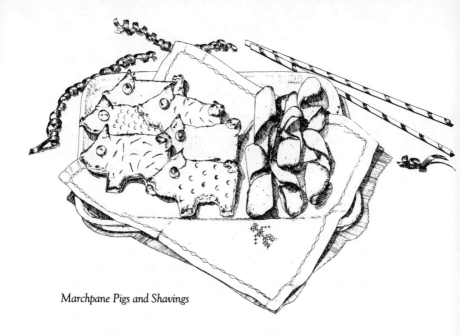

Marchpane Pigs and Shavings

claims that the confection was first made by medieval nuns in France. When freshly made the mixture is soft and pliable and it is ideal for moulding into an endless variety of shapes — fruit, flowers or even people. Food colouring can be worked into the marzipan to give the colour required and can be diluted and brushed on to give shading and the impression of ripeness. Small marzipan fruit are especially attractive, and can be eaten just as they are as sweets or petits fours or they make a pretty decoration for cakes and rich puddings.

8oz (225g) ground almonds	*1 egg white*
4oz (115g) caster sugar	*2 teaspoons (2×5ml) lemon juice*
4oz (115g) icing sugar	*Food colouring*

Mix the almonds with the caster sugar. Add the sieved icing sugar and stir in the egg white lightly whisked with the lemon juice. Mix well to make a smooth, firm dough. The marzipan is now ready for use; as an almond paste for decorating cakes or for colouring and shaping as you wish. Wrapped in a plastic bag and kept cold the marzipan will store well for several weeks.

MARCHPANE · PIGS

Hidden in a glade in Claremont landscape garden* near Esher is a large stone boar with curly hair on its back. It is traditional to kiss the snout of this boar for good luck. That done, one lovely late autumn day, I returned home and devised some sweetmeats based on the Claremont boar. In folklore the pig is associated with good fortune so a small marzipan pig might well be added to a box of homemade sweets.

8oz (225g) ground almonds
3oz (85g) caster sugar
1oz (30g) candied orange peel,
    finely chopped
Few drops of orange flower water

1oz (30g) blanched almonds,
    toasted and chopped
1 egg, separated
Icing sugar

Mix the ground almonds with the caster sugar in a bowl and stir in the candied peel, chopped almonds and orange flower water. Whisk the egg white lightly and add sufficient to make a soft malleable dough. Roll out the marzipan on a board lightly dusted with icing sugar until 1/4in (5mm) thick. Use a pig-shaped cutter or cut round a cardboard template to cut out as many pigs as possible. Make a curly tail and eyes from the trimmings. Brush the pigs with egg yolk and toast lightly under a hot grill until golden brown. Cool on a wire rack.

STUFFED · DATES

Fresh dates stuffed with homemade marzipan are very good indeed. A few in a small box, prettily wrapped, make a delightful present.

8oz (225g) fresh dates
4oz (115g) prepared marzipan (see
    pages 79-80)

A splash of rum or brandy (optional)
16–20 blanched almonds, toasted
A little icing sugar

Use a small sharp knife carefully to remove the stone from each date. Try to keep the date in one piece but if the date falls into two pieces this does not matter too much. Knead the marzipan until soft, if you wish working in the rum or brandy as you do so. Divide the marzipan between the dates, shaping each piece to fit into the date in place of the stone but leave some of the filling showing. Press an almond into the marzipan in each date. Lightly dust the dates with icing sugar and place each one in a paper case.

COTTAGE · CANDY

Pink and white striped peppermint sticks shaped like walking sticks are still popular at Christmas in North America. They are rarely seen in Britain these days.

1lb (450g) golden syrup
1/2pt (300ml) water
Oil of peppermint

Pink food colouring
A little icing sugar

Measure the syrup and water into a heavy-based pan and stir until well mixed. Boil steadily until the mixture reaches 280°F (137°C) or

the *soft crack* stage. Remove the pan from the heat and allow the syrup
to cool until it thickens. Turn the mixture on to a cold surface and
divide in two. Knead a drop or two of oil of peppermint into one half
and pull and fold the candy until it becomes opaque. In the same way
work a little pink food colouring into the remaining half of the candy
until it is pale pink. Make each piece of candy into a long thin sausage
and twist the two colours together. Cut into 6in (15cm) lengths and
curve one end of each length to resemble a walking stick or 'candy
cane'. Set aside to harden. Dust the cottage candy with icing sugar
and store in an air-tight container.

WINNIE·THE·POOH · POPCORN

The most famous bear in children's literature would no doubt
appreciate this quick and scrumptious way of making popcorn. Children love popping corn and their look of amazement at the transforma-
tion in a handful of corn kernels when you lift the lid from the pan is
always a delight.

A little mild salad oil
4oz (115g) popping corn
4oz (115g) butter
4oz (115g) honey

A little ground cinnamon for those
    children with more sophisticated
    tastes

Pour the oil into a large heavy-based saucepan and heat over moderate heat. Add the corn and raise the heat until the corn starts to pop.
Remove from the heat for 1 minute and place a lid on the pan.
Replace over high heat and when the corn starts to pop shake the pan
keeping it over the heat until the popping noise ceases. Take the pan
from the heat and tip the now fluffy popcorn into a large mixing bowl.
Wipe the pan free of oil with kitchen paper. Melt the butter with the
honey in the pan. Boil the mixture for 2 minutes then pour the syrup
over the popcorn and toss until evenly coated with the honey mixture. Eat straightaway or store in an air-tight plastic box.

ROSE · PETAL · FONDANTS

Pale pink rose fondants are sometimes decorated with a small crystallised rose petal, made a day ahead so that they are completely dry.

1 1/2lb (700g) cube sugar
1/2pt (300ml) cold water
Large pinch cream of tartar

Rosewater
Pink food colouring
Crystallised rose petals (see below)

Dissolve the sugar in the water in a heavy-based pan over medium
heat. Add the cream of tartar. Raise the heat and boil steadily until
the syrup reaches 237°F (114°C) or the *soft ball* stage. Pour the syrup
into a mixing bowl and allow to cool until luke-warm. Then beat with

a wooden spoon until white and stiff. Turn the paste on to the working surface and knead in a little rosewater and pink food colouring. Knead well until thoroughly mixed. Take a teaspoon of the paste, shape into a ball and flatten slightly. Place the fondants on greaseproof paper and leave in a warm place for 2–3 hours to harden.

Crystallised rose petals
Choose freshly fallen rose petals or pull those from a newly opened rose, preferably red or pink. Brush both sides of each petal with lightly whisked white of egg and then dust with caster sugar. Place the petals on a sheet of greaseproof paper on a wire rack. Leave in a warm place for some hours until the petals are completely dry. If very small the crystallised petals may be used whole, otherwise use scissors to cut the petals into small pieces. To decorate the fondants, press one petal on top of each as soon as they are made, then leave to harden.

ALMACK
This sweetmeat is a form of fruit pastille which sets like a firm jelly.

1lb (450g) apples   *¼pt (150ml) water*
1lb (450g) pears   *2lb (900g) sugar*
1lb (450g) plums

Peel and core the apples and pears. Slice both fruits into a pan. Add the plums, halved and stoned, and the water. Bring to the boil and simmer the fruit until tender. Purée the contents of the pan in a food processor or by sieving the mixture. Return the purée to the pan and add the sugar. Cook, stirring, over moderate heat until the sugar is dissolved. Raise the heat and cook, stirring now and again, until the mixture is thick and almost coming away from the pan. Spread the mixture on sheets of vegetable parchment in an even layer about ¼in (5mm) thick. Leave in a warm place for 1–2 days until the mixture is dry enough to be cut into squares or lozenges. Pack the almack into an air-tight box with paper between the layers.

APRICOT · CAKES
The earliest sweetmeats were made from fruit and nuts. Fruit paste dried in the sun or the oven was known as *tablet* and was popular in the sixteenth and seventeenth centuries. It was most commonly made from quinces or apricots but plums and pears were also used. The original of this recipe comes from a seventeenth-century manuscript recipe book of Dorset recipes. To make the apricot cakes with fresh apricots, cook double the weight of fruit with very little water, then purée and continue as in the recipe.

8oz (225g) dried apricots	*1–1½lb (450–700g) sugar*
¾pt (400ml) warm water	*1½oz (45g) caster sugar*

Soak the dried apricots in the warm water for 4 hours. Cook gently over a low heat for 20–30 minutes until completely tender. Purée the apricots and liquid in a food processor or sieve them. Measure the pulp and return to the pan with an equal weight of sugar. Stir over low heat until the sugar has dissolved. Raise the heat and cook the mixture, stirring from time to time, until thick enough to almost leave the sides of the pan. Turn into a lightly buttered non-stick baking tin and place in a very low oven for 1–2 hours or a warm room for 2–4 days until the paste is dry enough to be cut into squares. Roll the squares in caster sugar and arrange on a plate or in a pretty box.

SHAVINGS
By curving these sweets round the handle of a wooden spoon you create a spiral shape that resembles wood shavings.

1 egg white	*½oz (15g) cornflour*
4oz (115g) ground almonds	*2–3 tablespoons (2–3×15ml)*
5oz (140g) caster sugar	*double cream*

Lightly whisk the egg white and work in the ground almonds, sugar and cornflour. Beat in sufficient cream to make a smooth batter that is just thick enough to pipe. Spoon the mixture into a forcing bag fitted with a plain ½in (10mm) nozzle. Pipe strips of the mixture onto a baking sheet lined with non-stick baking paper. Bake in a moderate oven (375°F, 190°C; Gas Mark 5) for 5–6 minutes until the edges are turning brown. Remove from the oven and while still hot roll each strip around a buttered stick or handle of a wooden spoon in a spiral. As soon as the shavings are set, slide off and cool on a wire rack.

CHOCOLATE · ORANGE · TRUFFLES
For a more professional look roll truffles in chocolate chips or vermicelli and then place them in small paper cases.

4oz (115g) plain dessert chocolate	*1 tablespoon (1×15ml) orange juice*
2oz (55g) butter	*3oz (85g) ground almonds*
2 egg yolks	*1–2oz (30–55g) grated chocolate*
Grated zest of ½ orange	*or chocolate vermicelli*

Break the chocolate into pieces and melt with the butter in a bowl set over hot water. Remove the bowl from the heat and stir in the egg yolks and zest and juice of orange. Mix in the ground almonds to make a stiff paste. Set the bowl aside or stand it in cold water until the mixture is cold. Take a teaspoon of the mixture, shape into a ball and roll in the grated chocolate. If you wish, place into small paper cases.

CHOCOLATE-COATED · SWEETMEATS

If you plan to make sweets at home, possibly with children, this is a good way to start. Once you've melted the chocolate the bowl can be moved away from the cooker on to a table where children can work safely.

A selection of whole nuts, candied fruits, dried fruits (apricots, dates, quartered figs)

marshmallows, strips of candied peel (see below)
8oz (225g) plain dessert chocolate

Break the chocolate in pieces and melt in a bowl over hot water. Stir until smooth. Move the bowl to a working table. Use a long wooden stick or metal skewer or fork to hold the items to be coated. Dip in the melted chocolate until completely covered. Place on waxed paper or vegetable parchment and leave until the chocolate has set. Remove the sweets from the paper and place in paper cases or on fringed tissue paper in a box or dish.

CANDIED · PEEL

2 oranges
2 lemons

Cold water
8oz (225g) sugar

Wash the fruit well and cut in quarters. Remove the flesh and as much pith as possible from the peel. Place in a pan with cold water to cover and bring to the boil. Simmer for 1–1½ hours until tender. Pour ½pt (300ml) of the cooking liquid into a pan and dissolve the sugar in it. Add the drained peel and simmer for 45–60 minutes until the peel becomes clear as in marmalade. Drain well, then dry the peel in a low oven or a warm place for 3–4 hours. Use within one month or freeze.

ELIZA · ACTON'S · PALACE · BON-BONS

In *Modern Cookery for Private Families*, first published in 1845, Eliza Acton, the foremost cookery writer of the nineteenth century, gives a recipe for these sweets.

She takes fresh candied peel (above) cut into narrow strips. These are dipped in liquid barley sugar or caramel. Any caramel or toffee left over when making another recipe (for example toffee apples) is excellent for making these sweets. Place the caramel-coated candied peel on a lightly oiled plate or on waxed paper and set aside to harden. Remove from the paper and store in an air-tight container.

·Jams, Honeys· and Spreads

'Stands the church clock at ten to three?
And is there honey still for tea?'

For eight decades Rupert Brooke's famous lines about Grantchester have captured our imagination and the image of English afternoon tea. The tinkle of tea-cups, a table covered with a lace cloth, and thin bread and butter with potted ham or cucumber sandwiches, with a batch of scones, warm from the oven. The scones are split open and spread with strawberry jam or lemon curd, or, of course, honey. All this represents for many of us the essence of Englishness. Tea-time is a civilised time — a time to pause, to chatter and perhaps gossip over a cup of China or Indian tea. Above all it is a time to reflect.

Many of the recipes that follow make a small amount of jam or spread, just enough for tea, to take on a picnic, to send a potful in a tuck box — jam from home is always special.

FRESH · STRAWBERRY · JAM
This is an uncooked and 'instant' jam which is delicious served with hot scones and clotted cream. The raspberry version is equally good.

8oz (225g) ripe strawberries or
  raspberries
2–4 tablespoons (2–4 × 15ml)
  honey or caster sugar

½ orange, finely grated zest and
  juice

Mash the fruit with a fork and work in the honey or sugar and the zest and juice of the orange. Alternatively, purée all the ingredients in a blender or food processor until thick, taking care to stop before the mixture becomes too runny. Spoon the jam into a small pot and serve.

BANANA · JAM
Most children love this thick banana spread; it is delicious on hot toast or mixed with yoghurt.

1lb (450g) bananas
1¼pt (650ml) pineapple juice

1 lemon
12oz (340g) sugar, warmed

Strawberry Jam and Banana Jam

Peel and chop the bananas and cook with the pineapple juice and finely grated zest and juice of the lemon until soft. Add the sugar and cook, stirring over a low heat, until dissolved. Bring the mixture to the boil, lower the heat and simmer the jam for about 30 minutes. Pour into small warmed jars or a dish for serving as soon as the jam cools.

NECTARINE · AND · ORANGE · JAM

2¼lb (1kg) nectarines
1 large sweet orange
1lb (450g) sugar

2 tablespoons (2 × 15ml) peach
brandy (optional)
⅓ bottle liquid pectin

Pour boiling water over the nectarines, two at a time. Lift out and remove the thin skin and slice the fruit into a pan. Cut the peel very thinly from the orange and shred finely. Add to the fruit with the strained juice from the orange and cook gently over moderate heat, stirring to prevent sticking, for 5–10 minutes until the fruit is soft. Stir in the sugar until dissolved. Raise the heat and boil steadily for 8 minutes. Remove from the heat. Stir in the peach brandy if desired and add the pectin, stirring it in well. Pour the jam into small warm, dry jars or into a dish for serving.

LACOCK · APRICOT · JAM

Dried apricot jam can be made at any time of the year. This recipe comes from a booklet of tea-time recipes collected by Freda Murray when she ran the King John's Hunting Lodge Tea Rooms in the beautiful National Trust village of Lacock*, a few miles south of Chippenham in Wiltshire.

1lb (450g) dried apricots (not the
   pre-soaked kind)
4pt (2.25L) boiling water

3½lb (1.5kg) sugar, warmed
4oz (115g) blanched almonds,
   halved

If necessary wash the apricots well and turn into a mixing bowl.
Cover with the boiling water and leave to soak for 48 hours. Turn
into a pan and simmer the fruit very slowly for 1 hour. Add the sugar
and stir, over a low heat, until dissolved. Boil steadily until the jam
reaches 220°F (110°C) or a set is reached. Remove from the heat, stir
in the almonds and pour into warm, dry jars. Cover and label.

ANGEL'S · HAIR · JAM

In the nineteenth century this bright orange jam made from carrots
was very popular. I use it as a filling in tarts and sponge cakes. Or serve
it folded into whipped cream and spread between two layers of crisp
hazelnut meringue.

2lb (900g) tender carrots
½pt (300ml) water

2lb (900g) sugar
2 lemons

Peel the carrots and shred them finely into a pan. Add the water and
cook the carrots until tender. Stir in the sugar and the finely grated
zest and juice of the lemons until dissolved. Bring the mixture to the
boil and cook until the jam reaches 220°F (110°C) or a set is reached.
Pour into small dry, warm jars. Cover and label.

CINNAMON · HONEY · BUTTER

This is a quickly prepared alternative to plain honey which is delicious
spread on hot toast or scones.

2oz (55g) unsalted butter
4oz (115g) set honey

¼ teaspoon (¼×5ml) ground
   cinnamon

Cream the butter until soft. Gradually beat in the honey and cinnamon until thoroughly mixed and spreadable. Spoon into a small pot
or bowl for serving.

ST · CLEMENT'S · CURD

Homemade fruit curds are one of the oldest preserves. They do not
keep for months like jam and are best eaten within three weeks. For
the best flavour use a china or glass bowl and a wooden or plastic
spoon. Metal implements can impair the lovely flavour.

1 lemon
1 orange
4oz (115g) caster sugar

2 eggs
4oz (115g) unsalted butter

Wash and dry the fruit. Grate the zest from both fruits into a bowl placed over simmering water. Add the strained juice, sugar and eggs. Cook, stirring, for 10–15 minutes until the mixture is thick enough to coat the back of a spoon. Remove the bowl from the heat and gradually beat in the butter, adding it in small pieces. Spoon the curd into a small pot or jar. Cover and label and store in the refrigerator.

FAIRY · BUTTER

This is Elizabeth Raffald's eighteenth-century recipe for a delicate sweet butter flavoured with orange flower water. The butter is delightful spread on thin bread or as a filling in a sponge cake.

4oz (115g) butter   *4 egg yolks, hard-boiled*
2oz (55g) caster sugar   *Orange flower water to taste*

Cream the butter with the caster sugar until light and fluffy. Add the egg yolks rubbed through a nylon sieve and beat until smooth. Mix in sufficient orange flower water to give a delicate flavour. Spoon into a small dish for serving.

CASHEW · NUT · BUTTER

Most nuts can be finely ground to make a spreadable butter. Cashew nuts, which have a more subtle and attractive flavour than peanuts, make an excellent savoury spread.

4oz (115g) shelled cashew nuts   *Salt*
Cold water

Spread the nuts in a single layer on a baking sheet. Toast under a hot grill until golden. Remove and leave until cool. Pound the nuts in a mortar or chop finely in a food processor. Add sufficient cold water to make a spreadable paste. Mix until the nut butter has the smoothness you require. Season to taste with salt. Spoon into a small pot to serve.

PUMPKIN · CREAM

This thick pumpkin spread makes an excellent filling for pies and tarts or served for spreading on toasted buns or muffins.

2lb (900g) pumpkin, peeled, seeded   *3/4 teaspoon (3/4 × 5ml) ground*
    and diced   *ginger*
1/4pt (150ml) water   *1/2 teaspoon (1/2 × 5ml) ground*
1 1/2–2lb (700–900g) sugar   *nutmeg*
1 orange   *4oz (115g) unsalted butter*
1 lemon
3/4 teaspoon (3/4 × 5ml) ground
    mace

Cook the pumpkin with the water over a low to moderate heat until tender. Raise the heat and evaporate any surplus liquid. Purée the pumpkin in a food processor or push through a fine nylon sieve. Return the purée to the pan allowing 12oz (350g) sugar to each 1lb (450g) of purée. Stir in the finely grated zest and juice of the orange and the lemon, the mace, ginger and nutmeg and bring to the boil. Cook, stirring, for 15–20 minutes until thick. Add the butter in small pieces and stir in until melted. Spoon the mixture into small jars. Cover and label. This pumpkin cream should be stored in a very cold place and be eaten within 2 months.

ANCHOVY · BUTTER

In Charles Dickens' *Little Dorrit* afternoon tea was served. 'Arthur . . . repaired to his mother's room, where Mr. Casby and Flora had been taking tea, anchovy paste, and hot buttered toast.'

Anchovy butter is a more refined version of anchovy paste. It is very good spread straight on to hot toast, each slice, ideally, browned on a toasting fork before the fire.

1³/₄oz (45g) tin anchovy fillets   *Lemon juice*
4oz (115g) unsalted butter   *Cayenne pepper*

Rinse the anchovy fillets in tepid water and drain on kitchen paper. Pound the fillets in a mortar or chop finely in a food processor. Add the butter in small pieces with a dash of lemon juice and mix to a smooth paste. Season with a pinch of cayenne pepper and spoon the mixture into a small pot. Smooth level and chill until needed.

POTTED · HAM

The well-run Victorian and Edwardian household not only produced all its own preserves and jams, it also potted meat and cheese. Potted meat was served with hot toast at tea-time or for a late evening supper. This potted ham is simple to make and is extremely good.

8oz (225g) ham, free of fat   *A good pinch of grated nutmeg*
4oz (115g) unsalted butter   *Cayenne pepper*
A good pinch of ground mace

Dice the meat and pound it in a mortar or chop it finely in a food processor. Add the butter, cut in pieces, and blend together. Season to taste with mace, nutmeg and cayenne pepper. Spoon the mixture into a small pot or jar and smooth the top. Chill until ready to serve. Potted ham stores well in the refrigerator for up to 1 week. To keep potted ham in a cool larder the top must be sealed with a layer of clarified butter.

·Beverages·

'What's inside it?' asked the Mole, wriggling with curiosity.
'There's cold chicken inside it,' replied the Rat briefly;
'coldtonguecoldhamcoldbeefpickledgherkinssaladfrenchrolls
cresssandwichespottedmeatgingerbeerlemonadesodawater —'
'O stop, stop,' cried the Mole in ecstasies: 'This is too much!'

Whether Rat did, in fact, provide even more drinks for the riverside
picnic with Mole, we shall never know. Kenneth Grahame, the
author, did not tell us. No matter, because homemade fizzy ginger
beer and lemonade clinking with ice cubes are delightful drinks for a
picnic on a summer's day. The ice cubes themselves can be made even
more appealing by freezing a sprig of mint, a sliver of lemon or a
cocktail cherry in the centre of each. Children enjoy watching the
ice cube melt and its frozen contents float to the surface.

In the past children's drinks differed little from those of their
parents. Wine or sack even when watered down is still fairly strong
liquor. In the late nineteenth century at a children's ball in London
the only drink on offer to the young guests was a champagne cup!

Kenneth Grahame wrote *Wind in the Willows* at the height of the
Edwardian era when the picnic was taken seriously; it was a leisurely
way to spend a day or evening with the added pleasure of an informal
meal. To children the freedom to run and play and eat sitting on the
grass must have been especially welcome. For everyone the Edwardian picnic offered a foretaste of the more relaxed way of life that was
to come later in the century.

MINT · LEMONADE

Handful of mint leaves	*Ice cubes*
2 tablespoons (2 × 15ml) sugar	*Slices of lemon*
3 lemons	*Sprigs of mint*
1pt (500ml) boiling water	

Lightly crush the mint leaves and place in a jug or bowl with the
sugar. Wash and dry the lemons and mince coarsely. Add the mush
to the mint and pour over the boiling water. Cover and set aside for
1–2 hours until cool. Strain into glasses and top up with ice cubes.
Add a slice of lemon, a sprig of mint and serve.

*Mint Lemonade, Iced Russian Chocolate and
Strawberry Shrub*

WILMA'S · GRAPE · RICKEY

As children we always found my mother's grape cocktail convincingly
like wine — in looks anyway.

*1 bottle of red grape juice
4–6 tablespoons (4–6 × 15ml)
    lime juice or cordial
Sugar to taste (optional)*

*Sparkling mineral water or
    lemonade
Iced cubes (see page 91)*

Mix the grape juice with the lime juice and add a little sugar if
thought necessary. Dilute with sparkling water and serve over ice
cubes in glasses.

STRAWBERRY · SHRUB

Shrub is an old country word for cordial and comes from the Arabic
for drink, *sharbah*. This pink strawberry syrup (which also makes an
excellent sauce for ice cream) is a cooling fizzy drink.

*1 ¹/₂lb (700g) fresh strawberries
6–8oz (170–225g) sugar
Lemon juice*

*Ice cubes
Soda water*

Hull the strawberries, wash them quickly in cold water and drain
well. Place them in a pan with half the sugar. Bring to the boil, stirring until the sugar is dissolved. Simmer for 2 minutes and lightly
mash the fruit to extract all the juice. Strain the fruit through a fine
nylon sieve, pressing the fruit gently. Add the remaining sugar to the
liquid and stir until dissolved . Add lemon juice to taste and set the
syrup aside to cool.

To serve, pour some syrup into each glass, add ice cubes and top up
with soda water. Serve straightaway while the drink effervesces.

ORANGE · SQUASH

3 oranges
1 lemon
2pt (1.25L) water

1lb (450g) sugar
1oz (30g) citric acid

Wash and dry the fruit. Squeeze out the juice and reserve. Discard the pips and chop the fruit skins in a food processor or mincer. Turn the pulp into a pan and add the water. Bring to the boil and simmer for 5 minutes. Strain the liquid into a jug and stir in the sugar until dissolved. Allow to cool, then add the reserved juice and the citric acid. Bottle and label, and store in the refrigerator for up to 3 weeks. To serve, dilute with water or soda water.

SPICED · ORANGE · DRINK

1 small orange
6 cloves
1 tablespoon (1 × 15ml) honey

Juice of 1 or 2 oranges
Boiling water

Wash and dry the orange and stick the cloves into the skin. Place on a baking dish and bake in a hot oven for 10–15 minutes. Remove from the oven and slice thinly into a jug. Add the honey and the orange juice. Pour on boiling water and stir until the honey is dissolved. Place a teaspoon in a glass to prevent it cracking and add the strained orange drink. Serve straightaway.

BLACKCURRANT · SYRUP

For a cool summer drink dilute this syrup with ice cubes and soda water. In winter mix the syrup with hot water and a splash of rum if appropriate.

1lb (450g) blackcurrants
2pt (1.25L) water

1lb (450g) sugar

Quickly rinse the blackcurrants in cold water. Drain and remove any leaves and the larger stalks. Turn the fruit into a pan with the water and slowly bring to the boil. Stir in the sugar until dissolved. Boil for 5 minutes. Strain into warm, dry sterilised bottles. Seal and label. Store in the refrigerator.

FRUIT · CORDIAL

1 grapefruit (optional)
2 large oranges
1 lemon

1/2oz (15g) tartaric acid
1lb (450g) sugar
2pt (1.25L) boiling water

Wash the fruit well. Cut into quarters and mince or chop in a food processor until quite fine. Pour the mush into a bowl. Stir in the tartaric acid and sugar. Add the boiling water and stir until the sugar has dissolved. Cover and leave for 2–3 hours or until cool. Strain the liquid into a bottle. Seal, label and store in the refrigerator.

To serve, pour a generous measure of the cordial into a glass and top up with cold or hot water.

GINGER · BEER

This is an excellent speedy recipe for ginger beer because the drink is ready after 3 days.

2 lemons	1 tablespoon (1 × 15ml) ground
1lb (450g) sugar	ginger
1½ teaspoons (1½ × 5ml) cream	8pt (4.5L) boiling water
of tartar	1 tablespoon (1 × 15ml) dried yeast

Wash and dry the lemons. Slice thinly and place in a large heatproof bowl or plastic bucket. Add the sugar, cream of tartar and the ginger. Pour over the boiling water. When lukewarm add the yeast. Cover and leave for 24 hours. Strain into screw-top jars or bottles. Drink after a further 2 days and within the week. If left longer there may be a risk of explosions!

MILK · SHAKES

Milk shakes are quick and easy to make. Children regard them as the ultimate luxury and each foaming glass is greeted with delight.

RASPBERRY · OR · STRAWBERRY · MILK · SHAKE

per person:

1 glass chilled milk	A little raspberry or strawberry
1 scoop raspberry or strawberry	syrup
ice-cream	

Whisk the milk with the ice-cream and pour into a glass. Pour a little raspberry syrup on top and serve with two drinking straws.

PINEAPPLE · COOLER

per person:

1 glass chilled pineapple juice	2 scoops vanilla ice-cream

Whisk the pineapple juice with half the ice-cream. Pour into a glass and add the other scoop of ice-cream. Serve with two straws and a spoon to eat the ice-cream at the bottom of the glass.

INDEX

ICED · RUSSIAN · CHOCOLATE

1 mug hot cocoa
1/3 mug hot black coffee
Vanilla-flavoured sugar to taste
Few ice cubes

2 tablespoons (2 × 15ml) whipped
   cream
A little grated chocolate

Mix the cocoa with the coffee and sweeten to taste with the vanilla sugar. Cool, then chill in the refrigerator. Divide between two glasses and add 1 or 2 ice cubes. Top with whipped cream and chocolate.

CAMBRIDGE · MILK · PUNCH

This nineteenth-century drink is described by Edward Spencer in *Cakes and Ale* as a 'fairly good boys' beverage, there being absolutely "no offence in it".' I leave you to decide at what age boys should be offered this inoffensive drink! The cider cup from Oxford (see below) may be preferable.

1pt (500ml) milk
12 lumps sugar
Strip of lemon rind

1 egg yolk
1 tablespoon (1 × 15ml) cold milk
2 tablespoons (2 × 15ml) brandy
4 tablespoons (4 × 15ml) rum

Warm the milk with the sugar and the lemon rind. Simmer gently for 15 minutes to extract the flavour from the rind. Remove from the heat and discard the rind. Blend the egg yolk with the cold milk, brandy and rum and whisk into the warm milk until frothy. Serve straightaway.

ORIEL · COLLEGE · CIDER · CUP

This is a mid-nineteenth century recipe for a spiced cup. For younger people it may be diluted with apple juice or lemonade.

1/2oz (15g) cloves
1/2oz (15g) allspice berries
1 stick of cinnamon
2pt (1.25L) water
4pt (2.5L) sweet cider

2–3 slices lemon
1/2 wineglass Noyeau or Crème de
   Noyaux
Sugar to taste
Well-toasted bread, cut in squares

First of all, prepare the spiced liquid. Place the spices in a pan with the water. Bring to the boil, lower the heat and simmer very gently for 4–5 hours until the flavour is extracted from the spices. Strain the liquid into a screw-top jar or bottle and set aside to cool.

To make the cider cup, measure 2 wine glasses of the spice liquid into a large jug. Add the cider, slices of lemon and the Noyeau. Stir in sugar according to taste and finally float the toast on top.